K

THE ARENA OF RACISM

D0222931

DATE DUE

NOV 2 8 1997	
MAR - 2 1998	
MAY - 8 1998	
OCT 1 4 1998	
MAR 1 1 1999	
OCT - 4 1999	

BRODART	Cat. No. 23-221

Theory, Culture & Society

Theory, Culture & Society caters for the resurgence of interest in culture within contemporary social science and the humanities. Building on the heritage of classical social theory, the book series examines ways in which this tradition has been reshaped by a new generation of theorists. It will also publish theoretically informed analyses of everyday life, popular culture, and new intellectual movements.

Recent volumes include:

THE ARENA
OF RACISM

Michel Wieviorka

Translated by Chris Turner

SAGE Publications

London • Thousand Oaks • New Delhi

First published in English in 1995

Originally published in French as *L'Espace du Racisme* by Les
Éditions du Seuil, Paris
© Les Éditions du Seuil 1991

This translation is published with financial support from the French
Ministry of Culture

SAGE Publications Ltd
6 Bonhill Street
London EC2A 4PU

SAGE Publications Inc
2455 Teller Road
Thousand Oaks, California 91320

SAGE Publications India Pvt Ltd
32, M-Block Market
Greater Kailash – I
New Delhi 110 048

Published in association with *Theory, Culture & Society*, School of
Human Studies, University of Teesside

British Library Cataloguing in Publication data

A catalogue record for this book is available from the British Library

ISBN 0 8039 7880 4
ISBN 0 8039 7881 2 (pbk)

Library of Congress catalog record available

Typeset by Photoprint, Torquay, Devon, UK
Printed in Great Britain by The Cromwell Press Ltd, Broughton
Gifford, Melksham, Wiltshire

to my parents

CONTENTS

ACKNOWLEDGEMENTS

This work charts a solitary journey, but one on which I have received much support, both intellectual and practical, all of it expressed with warmth.

My thanks go, first of all, to the director of the Centre d'analyse et d'intervention sociologiques (CADIS), Alain Touraine, and to the researchers of that institution to which I have always been happy to belong, beginning with François Dubet and Didier Lapeyronnie who, with Alain Touraine, read a first draft of this work and helped me to make various improvements to it. Thanks are also due to the members of the research team I formed to study the phenomena of racism in their most concrete manifestations: Philippe Bataille, Bernard Francq, Daniel Jacquin, Danilo Martuccelli, Angelina Peralva, Paul Zawadzki and Patricia Pariente who acted as assistant. Without the collective work of that team, the fruits of whose labours have now been published elsewhere,* the book would not have been what it is.

Lastly, my thanks go, again within CADIS, to Mireille Coustance, Jacqueline Blayac, Jacqueline Longerinas and, most particularly, to Lidia Meschy, whose assistance was crucial in the final preparation of the manuscript.

The working group on racism, where we met regularly in a spirit of friendship, was a source of stimulation and discussion which meant a great deal to me; I therefore thank Jeanne Ben Brika, Jean-Claude Monet, Charles Rojzman, Dominique Schnapper, Étienne Schweisguth, Pierre-André Taguieff and, more especially, Nonna Mayer and Gérard Lemaine for their comments on the first version of this work.

I also thank my sister Annette who also suggested crucial changes and corrections, and Patrick Rotman for his trust and friendship.

Lastly, this book, which was built up step by step over two years as I gave my weekly seminars at the École des hautes études en sciences sociales, owes much to the exacting curiosity of my students.

---

* M. Wieviorka (ed.), *La France raciste*, Seuil, Paris, 1992.

PREFACE

This book arises out of an anxiety, related to the time and place of its composition. Is it not the case that, at the end of the twentieth century, France is becoming a racist society? Is it not, indeed, threatened by a wave of racism which has already taken a foothold, in the shape of the Front national, at the political level? The term 'racism' is, admittedly, not necessarily the most appropriate. It is a term which is even misapplied at times to populism, xenophobia or a sombre nationalism – and the factual data, the statistics on racism, as they appear for example in the results of a survey carried out recently at the Prime Minister's behest, may seem quite small-scale.[1]

Yet we have good reason to be worried. The immigration issue, which has assumed an important place in current debates, is fraught with racist connotations; against a background of urban change and a school system in crisis, a form of segregation has crept up on us which would have been unthinkable ten or fifteen years ago; racist prejudices are more and more openly expressed, as though the taboos and prohibitions, including the legal ones, had been lifted, particularly where people from the Maghreb are concerned; an anti-black racism is developing, which is active and visible wherever Africans, Haitians or – very French – West Indians are becoming mingled with, or supplanting, earlier waves of immigrants; the presence of anti-semitism is attested by an increasing amount of written material (it is not easy to understand how this can be printed and circulated with such ease), generated around a series of headline-making incidents – Aix-les-Bains, Carpentras, etc.[2] – or as part of the so-called 'revisionist' thinking which denies the existence of the gas chambers.

The present upsurge in racism, both in France and in other European societies, is not dissociable from a significant social mutation. Only yesterday, the 'social question' was predominant, that question being shaped by struggles conducted, directly or indirectly, in the name of the labour movement. Only yesterday, the existence of cultural or religious particularisms seemed subordinate to universal values, to a single conception of progress, to states more or less capable of speaking simultaneously the language of modernity and that of the nation, capable also of integrating foreigners and of assimilating them in the short or long term. Modernity is so badly shaken today that we hear talk of post-modernity; the idea of class relations has become archaic; states seem increasingly powerless to maintain the old models of integration; and everywhere communal identities, whether defined in religious, ethnic, regional, cultural, historical or, most importantly, national terms, are emerging or being reinforced.

This is the context in which the question of the current spread of racism must be posed. The space of that racism is expanding as the social relations which arose out of industrialization, particularly in its Taylorist phase, are coming to an end, as all kinds of non-social identities are asserting themselves, and as the capacity of the political authorities and intellectuals to combine the universality of progress and reason and the specificity of their nation in a single conception is giving way.

But it is not sufficient merely to postulate a link between racism and social change: we have to find the means to test this hypothesis; we have to develop or assemble the concepts which will enable us to establish the relationship between the various expressions of racism in a society and the work [*travail*] of that society both on itself and in its relations with other social ensembles.

The present work is devoted to this end. Our aim is not, then, to account directly for the upsurge of racism threatening France or Europe. We have a logically prior concern, which is the construction of the necessary instruments for understanding this type of phenomenon. And this implies stepping back somewhat from contemporary French or European experience and endeavouring to avoid proposing an *ad hoc* theory or, in other words, getting caught in the toils of ethnocentrism.

II

The development of ideas and research is, to a large extent, dependent on the national contexts within which it takes place. This is why one should not be too surprised at the backwardness of France where sociological studies of racism are concerned.

The French intellectual tradition is, admittedly, a vigorous one, whether we are speaking of the study of racist ideas and ideologies (into which Pierre-André Taguieff and Étienne Balibar have injected some fresh thinking), political science (particularly in the shape of the CEVIPOF's research on the Front national),[3] social psychology, psychoanalysis, history, political philosophy, ethnology or even the engagement on the part of the 'hard' sciences, beginning with biology and its critique of racial categorizations. But the silence of sociology contrasts starkly with what we find in other social sciences. Not so very long ago, Roger Bastide had a determining influence on the formation of Brazilian sociology and was regarded as an authority on the subject of racism, Albert Memmi produced some fine analyses of colonial racism, and Colette Guillaumin published a key work on racist ideology.[4] But over the last fifteen or twenty years France seems to have been struck down by sociological aphasia in this field, as if its researchers were reluctant to face up to the racist tendencies affecting their own society here and now. It is not that there is a lack of interest in the victims or targets of racism; the existence of the sociology of immigration, undistinguished (but for a few exceptions) as it may seem, proves that this is not the case.[5] But the production of racism itself, the social relations and changes it feeds on, have barely been studied, and there has been far more denunciation of the evil than real analysis of it.

In other societies, the intellectual ferment is less brilliant, but there is more soundly based knowledge and the social and political debates stand on firmer ground. It does not take very long to read all the strictly sociological literature devoted to this subject in recent times in France; by contrast, the wealth of American publications on the topic is impressive, and the best of these, sometimes dating back to the 1930s and 1940s, have never been translated – even partially – into French, which is something a classic like Gunnar Myrdal's work on the 'American dilemma' surely deserves.[6]

There is also a striking contrast between France and Britain, where a critical sociology of racism has developed in the last twenty years, giving rise to a large number of empirical studies and also some important theoretical debates.

These remarks should not be taken in isolation from a matter we alluded to above: the great mutation in which classic industrial society is breaking down and the models of integration of modernity and the nation are losing their force. France is, in fact, only now discovering the debates and tensions which have affected Britain over a much longer period. We are novices in relation to these problems, which are new to us (intercultural relations, ethnicity), and, where British sociologists analyse themes which forced their presence upon their society long before they began to emerge in ours, we are still hesitant to resort to a vocabulary which is foreign to our political culture (ethnic minorities, race relations).[7] I am not seeking prematurely to assert here that France is sliding towards the British model and, thence, towards an American 'non-melting-pot' model of pluri-ethnicity and racism; we are only at the beginning of a process and we know nothing yet of its future development. But we can assert, none the less, that the backwardness of French sociology where contemporary racism is concerned has to do in large measure with the novel or very recent character of these social problems with which other societies have been familiar, in the various forms specific to those societies, for many years.

III

Racism, which is a global phenomenon and one of considerable historical density, is sometimes defined very broadly as being synonymous with exclusion or the rejection of otherness. In this work, we shall keep to a stricter definition, demanding that, before we speak of racism, the idea of (some sort of) link should be present between the – physical, genetic or biological – attributes or heredity of an individual (or group) and the intellectual and moral characteristics of that individual (or group). The reader may, of course, be expecting a more elaborate definition. Let us simply say that this work, in its attempt to construct racism as an object, is in itself – in its totality – an attempt at a definition.

Two experiences, more than others, will mark out the space of our analyses and constitute two basic poles between which our thinking will constantly move, thus preventing it from becoming too limited or particular in its focus: on the one hand, the American experience, which is that of a racism rooted in the social structure and directed against what is, to a very large extent, a dominated population – the blacks – and, on the other, the European experience of anti-semitism, which is much more difficult to relate to a situation in which the Jew could be seen as a dominated social figure. This classic pair will not be the only reference point for our thinking, but it will play an essential role, if only by preventing us from too rapidly postulating the unity of the phenomenon and by forcing us to account for what are sometimes very profound differences between the two experiences.

In proceeding in this way, we are in danger of creating a misunderstanding or ambiguities, which we would perhaps do well to dispel right away. We are not aiming here to advance a theory of anti-black racism, nor of anti-semitism, nor indeed of the two, and we do not take any position at the outset in the important debate which ranges those who regard anti-semitism as a kind of racism against those who, by contrast, stress its specificity, which, in their view, makes it irreducible to the simple notion of racism.

If we organize our work very broadly around these two major experiences, we do so in fact for their exemplary character, which enables us to identify processes, to describe them and, hence, to formalize them better than other experiences would allow. That these processes belong analytically to a single family seems to us undeniable – and in this we tend, therefore, towards regarding anti-semitism as one modality of racism. But the idea that it is necessary, in order to bring out the nature of these processes, to focus on two historical experiences and not one tends in the opposite direction. Our work does not enable us, then, to take up any firm position in this debate; its very conception is opposed to such a thing. But since it is far more concerned with mechanisms and logics of action than with explaining concrete situations, and since it is more analytical than historical, we shall regard anti-semitism as falling within the broader ambit of racism.

The reader may well be surprised, more generally, by the scant attention paid to the many other forms of racism. But the answer here will be the same. We do not under-estimate the virulence of racism when it affects other groups than the Jews or blacks in America, and we are quite aware that they too are entirely capable of adopting racist positions; we are quite aware of the degree to which, in a country like our own, hatred of Arabs and fear of Islam can slide beyond cultural rejection into racism. It is not our objective here, however, to examine the sites and objects, past and present, of racist contempt, inferiorization or exclusion, but to produce the instruments which make such an examination possible.

IV

In the attempt to develop analytical tools, we have everything to gain from the work of our predecessors, both from examining their advances and the dead-ends they may have run into. The first part of this book therefore proposes to take stock of the most important available knowledge. It does not aim to reconstitute a history of thinking on the subject – that would be beyond the scope of this work – but to reconstitute some of the principal stages (those which are, in our view, most decisive) in the research, the framing of new perspectives and the debates which, for more than a century, have been concerned, in one way or another, with racism. This shows us, most importantly, how difficult it is to construct racism as an object, how hesitantly and slowly sociology has developed. After first playing its part in the invention of racism, then taking up the study of 'race relations', this discipline finds it very difficult, even today, to break radically with debates on race and confront, in their unity, the discourses, thinking and behaviour which make up racism.

The operation which consists in highlighting physical or biological attributes which are supposed to shape behaviour, culture or personality or to justify relations of domination, exclusion, persecution or destruction finds concrete expression in many different forms, all of these so many elementary forms of racism. Part Two of this book examines these forms one by one in the light of two analytical distinctions. It looks at prejudice, segregation, discrimination and violence as empirical categories which can function at different – political or infra-political – levels, as categories linked, in each particular case, to one of two distinct logics, the one being a logic of inferiorization, which aims to ensure the racialized group receives unequal treatment, the other a logic of differentiation, which tends to set it apart and, in extreme cases, expel or exterminate it.

The unity of racism is to be found neither in its elementary forms, where it is concretely manifested in extremely diverse ways, nor in its levels and logics of action, where it is possible and desirable to make analytic distinctions. It can only be seen if we shift the perspective to consider the phenomenon as an action. An action of a very particular kind, since it functions by the negation of all social relations and naturalizes or demonizes the racialized group at the same time as it, possibly, over-values the racializing group in terms which are themselves also not social or even cultural. And, above all, it is an action which can only spread under conditions which are fixed, quite irrespective of the significations it sets in motion, by the transformations affecting the social or communal actors in the particular society in question. Part Three of this book makes a very precise study of these transformations and the space they are liable to open up for racism and for its most concrete expressions.

The present work is, then, neither a treatise on, nor a conspectus of, the available knowledge, even though it attempts to cover what is most important in that knowledge. From this point of view, it has definite limitations. But it does offer a coherent theoretical framework, an integrated set of analytical instruments, a concentrated body of hypotheses and arguments. It seems to us that what it loses on the one hand, it gains on the other. In our view, what is most urgently required today is that we equip ourselves with the means to see more clearly into the processes which enable racism to spread in societies like our own. It is our hope that this book, written without haste, will be able to meet that challenge.

PART ONE
FROM RACE TO RACISM

INTRODUCTION

In fact, as a geneticist, I believed that, thanks to biology, I could help people see things more clearly by saying, 'You talk about race, but what does the word mean?' And I showed them it couldn't be defined without arbitrariness or ambiguity. . . . In other words, there is no scientific basis for the concept of *race* and, as a result, racism must disappear. A few years ago, I would have argued that in making that statement I had properly discharged my role as a scientist and a citizen. And yet, though there are no *races*, racism certainly exists![1]

Race, racism. The unhappy experience of Albert Jacquard, the scientist who believed he could settle a social problem with a rational demonstration, raises in a simple, almost naïve, way the question of the construction of the object we shall be studying from this point onwards. What Jacquard says, in substance, is this: even when the debate on human races has been resolved, that settles nothing. Racism now appears in all its nakedness and must be understood in terms of other conceptual categories than those of biology or genetics.

Perhaps we should resist somewhat the idea that the debate on the existence of races ought to be closed once and for all. The liveliness of the controversy on the heredity of intelligence – which is more than a century old and has recently been reconstructed by Gérard Lemaine and Benjamin Matelon[2] – or certain works on the genetics of populations and bio-anthropology enumerated by Alain de Benoist[3] might invite us to do so. But, whether or not it remains open, and even though it fuels the doctrinal and political thinking of racists and anti-racists, that debate cannot substitute for an analysis of racism. Would we expect sociologists of religion to take a stance on the existence of God, from which they might then derive explanations of faith or atheism, for example? The sociology of racism can only be developed by resolutely distancing itself from studies of, and polemics on, race: as Colette Guillaumin has so aptly put it, 'Imaginary and real races play the same role in the social process and are therefore identical as regards their social function: this is precisely the sociological problem.'[4]

Social thought has not always (to put it mildly) perceived – nor always wished to perceive – this necessary disjunction, which is the basis of any proper study of racism. It has taken a long time for clarity to emerge on this point and, even today, writers are often slow to distinguish clearly between issues of race and racism.

It has to be said that the very term 'racism' is of recent coinage and that we are so used to it today that we easily forget how remarkably new it is. Though the word 'race' entered the European vocabulary towards the end of the fifteenth century and became established as a scientific category in the nineteenth, the term 'racism' was not coined until the twentieth century, in the interwar period, and its widespread use dates only from the end of the Second World War and discovery of the horrors associated with the historical experience of Nazism. It has since not only broadened in application but has also become more commonplace, being used to describe many forms of hatred, contempt, rejection or discrimination. There is a ready association between racism and sexism (not without foundation, since sexism also rests on a physical or biological definition of woman), but reference is also frequently made to 'class racism', 'anti-youth' racism, etc., thus depriving the racist phenomenon proper of its specificity.* But, though the notion of racism is new, the phenomenon is older and social thought has taken an interest in it, even before it bore its present name, since the first half of the nineteenth century.

This is why, beginning in that period, we are going to examine the most important moments in social thought on this subject, choosing to look at writers whose *oeuvre* – or, in some cases, whose individual works – seem particularly significant or crucial. The distance between the periods in which some of these texts were written and the point where racism became an explicit notion raises a problem we shall not under-estimate: the problem of anachronism. We shall not, therefore, assess the thinking of a particular writer here in the light of later knowledge or events – as, for example, when nineteenth-century racist thinkers are read in terms of Nazi anti-semitism – but shall mark out stages, shifts, recastings of perspective within a history of ideas the guiding thread of which is provided by a central preoccupation: evaluating the various contributions to the development of a properly sociological perspective on racism.

---

* *Translator's note:* This is not so true of the English language, where terms derived on the same lines as racism are more often employed (e.g. ageism).

1
RACE AS EXPLANATORY PRINCIPLE

It has to be said very clearly from the outset: the social sciences have contributed a great deal to the invention of racism, to its formulation as doctrine and scholarly theory. Admittedly, the founders of those sciences do not all – far from it – deserve the epithet 'racist' as we understand it today. And even the pioneers of racial thinking – a precursor like Gobineau, for example – need to be evaluated with caution, given the extent to which events like the Nazi experience far exceed their conceptions and would perhaps have horrified them.

But the emerging social sciences accorded considerable importance to the notion of race. They often presented it as a category whereby social structure, social change or the movement of history could be understood, thus clearing the path for 'ideological' racism. We shall shortly meet some major figures, such as Alexis de Tocqueville or Max Weber, who had little truck with this perspective; and to some writers it is quite alien, or of no great moment or consequence, as in the work of Auguste Comte, who observes in his *Catéchisme positiviste* of 1852 that the different human races do not have the same brain, but does not develop any conclusions from this which merit the least suspicion of racism.

Our starting point is, however, a major intellectual phenomenon: the formation of ideas and doctrines which, far from helping us to constitute racism as an object of analysis, held up race as a principle for explaining social life and, particularly, for explaining history.

1. Europe and the idea of race

Must not the idea that there are superior and inferior races, and, particularly, the idea that race shapes culture and is at the base of social differences, be sought very far back in our past, at the primary source of modern European culture, namely among the Greeks of the Hellenic period – or at least in the Middle Ages? This hypothesis, advanced most notably by Christian Delacampagne,[1] acquires greater force as we move closer to the modern era and the spread of racism is linked with a number of founding moments, beginning with the discovery of other continents.

But, whatever the historical perspective adopted, most historians of the idea of racism see it as having developed most prodigiously in the nineteenth century, with that century's combination of colonialism, scientific and industrial development, urbanization, immigration, population movements and, at the same time, of individualization and the upsurge of nationalisms.

The social thinking on racist themes which then developed was not by any means the work of sociologists alone, there being few who defined themselves as such at the time. It formed, rather, out of an impressive convergence of all the fields of knowledge, with countless contributions from philosophers, theologians, anatomists, physiologists, historians and philologists, and also from writers, poets and travellers, the common basis being the principle of the classification of species, to which Linnaeus perhaps gave the most decisive formulation.[2]

Some, like Renan, were interested in the Aryan origins of the West and, as Maurice Olender, following Léon Poliakov, has recently reminded us, fashioned an opposition between Semites and Aryans which redounded to the theoretical advantage of the latter.[3] Others, like Gustave Le Bon, drew a distinction between the superior races, all of them Indo-European, and the primitive ones, between which intermediate, 'middle' races – chiefly the Chinese and the Semitic peoples – might be situated.[4] Arthur de Gobineau, in his celebrated *Essai sur l'inégalité des races humaines*, advanced the theme of degeneration as a result of the mixing of races; his thinking was pessimistic in tone since he regarded the strength of a nation or people as lying in its capacity to absorb other peoples or nations, but the consequence of this was intermixing and decadence, which meant that humanity was inescapably doomed.[5] It was Georges Vacher de Lapouge's aim to found an anthropo-sociology in which the obsessive fear of cross-breeding would be confirmed by positivistic, scientistic recourse to biology and physical anthropology.[6] But the reader should not conclude from the few famous names mentioned here that this was solely a French concern.

In Britain, Francis Galton, a cousin of Charles Darwin, drew on the consequences of his ideas on racial differences to promote a eugenics which was central to the earliest debates of the Sociological Society of London (and not only theirs) – debates in which figures as prestigious as Max Nordau, Bertrand Russell, Ferdinand Tönnies, George Bernard Shaw or H.G. Wells took part, though they did not necessarily subscribe to Galton's views.[7] But let us remember that an anachronistic attitude considerably distorts the perspective here since, in that period, before the world became aware of the horrors wrought by Nazism, eugenics was not the exclusive preserve of conservative thought and the extreme right. It was also a recourse for – and a cause espoused by – social reformers; it was ambivalent and subject to contradictory interpretations, some seeing it as a way of purifying the race, others as a means to bring progress to the whole of humanity.

In Germany, Otto Ammon developed a body of ideas comparable to that of Vacher de Lapouge, and Houston Stewart Chamberlain declared himself anxious – and not merely with regard to the Roman Empire – about 'racial chaos' and the growing influence of Jews in commerce, law, literature and politics. This Dresden-based son of a British admiral, who was also the son-in-law of Richard Wagner, may be regarded as a prophet of Nazism.[8] More generally, in the second half of the nineteenth century, the whole of Europe was gripped by a passion for measuring skulls and bones, for examining skin pigmentation, and the colour of eyes and hair. Everywhere, racial classifications were drawn up; a primarily religious anti-judaism gave way to a nationalistic, political anti-semitism; people became worried about degeneracy; and innumerable links were forged between an applied, scientific, technical knowledge and doctrines which did service for social thought. The climate of ideas in the nineteenth century was still far from having the quasi-fusional coherence that Nazism would bring. This is why we should not be surprised to find in the Jewish world in Western Europe – particularly in Second Empire France – intellectuals who did not hesitate to draw on physical anthropology, with its measurements and calibrations, to praise the Jewish race.[9] Knowledge of race was supposed to provide the key to moral, cultural and social differences, to explain the general evolution of humanity and provide a means to understand the sources of decadence, if not indeed to mitigate it.

This intellectual climate – numerous analyses of which are to be found in the extensive literature on the history of racism[10] – was to culminate in Nazism, which both drew to a great extent on the ideas generated in that climate and also offered an historically unique possibility for their pro-motion and implementation. Medicine, biology, chemistry, genetics, and also anthropology, ethnology, psychiatry, jurisprudence and demography would all play their part in the classification of populations and the scientific treatment of the Jews, half-Jews, quarter-Jews, Gypsies and mental patients (who were also 'racialized'), whether the aim was to identify and define them or to achieve their elimination.[11] And some of these disciplines, to which we may add archaeology,[12] would, into the bargain, provide the regime with historical legitimacy.

European racism was formed, even before it received its present name, out of the encounter with the Other – most often a dominated Other (colonialism) – and out of the invention, against the background of the rise of nationalisms, of modern anti-semitism – an invention in which a considerable number of thinkers were implicated and which Guillaume Marr put a name to in 1893.[13] But the expressions of that racism which have most rocked European, and even world, consciousness have con-cerned not so much the colonized peoples, even though many of them have been massacred or reduced to slavery, as the Jews, the victims of Nazism. This is probably why, in Europe, it was not until the rise of Nazism, and, most importantly, the end of the Second World War and the discovery of Auschwitz, that the social sciences – and not only those sciences – really carried through the revolution that turned racism into an object of analysis.

2. Alexis de Tocqueville and Max Weber

The theorists of race do not always take up radical positions. Some think that the inferior races can be improved by bringing progress, religion or education to them and develop what Pierre-André Taguieff terms a 'universalist-spiritualist racism',[14] the principal version of which is to be found in the colonial ideology of the French Third Republic as expressed by such men as Jules Ferry, or even socialists like Léon Blum, who spoke, for example, in the Chamber of Deputies in 1925 of the mission of the higher races and their duty to bring science and industry to the inferior races and raise them to a higher level of culture. Others turn the classical perspective around and invert its dominant postulate – that social life or mores are to be explained in terms of race. Thus Gabriel Tarde, who was extremely hostile to the theories of Vacher de Lapouge, which he criticized harshly, believed that every civilization in the end shapes its own race and hence that this latter is engendered by culture and society.[15]

We may note in passing that this perspective recurs much closer to our own day in Claude Lévi-Strauss's famous lecture of 1971, when he explains that:

> the cultural forms adopted in various places by human beings, their ways of life in the past or in the present, determine to a very great extent the rhythm of their biological evolution and its direction. Far from having to ask whether culture is or is not a function of race, we are discovering that race – or what is generally meant by this term – is one function among others of culture.[16]

Similarly, Ludwig Gumplowicz, a major influence on American sociology, describes the evolution of humanity as being governed by ruthless struggles which, as they end in the annihilation or dissolution of certain human groups, homogenize the dominant groups and transform them into races.[17] What he calls 'race' corresponds in fact to what we would today call nations and ethnic groups. Such writers certainly cannot be accused of racism. Similarly, one of the founding fathers of classical sociology, Émile Durkheim, the son of a rabbi, though he practically never wrote on the race question, none the less outlined an analysis of the functioning of racism within a society in the response he made in 1894 to a questionnaire on anti-semitism: 'when society is suffering, it feels the need to find someone to whom it can attribute the evil, someone on whom it can be avenged for its disappointment'.[18] The theory suggested by these few words is that of the scapegoating mechanism, which begins in a crisis or a dysfunctioning of society and targets a human group defined by a representation which has nothing, or very little, to do with its objective characteristics. This theory is of interest insofar as it lies at the root of an enormous body of interrelated work – to which we shall return below – which contends that racism should be analysed not in terms of relations between groups defined by race but – by-passing the idea of relation – by focussing on the racializing group, whose prejudices and behaviour can be explained without reference to the lived experience of contact with the racialized group or to the concrete reality of that group.

In fact, in the face of this upsurge of the idea of race, the most solid and stimulating positions are to be found not in Durkheim or Tarde, but in two other great figures of social thought: Alexis de Tocqueville and Max Weber. Both of these writers provide the basic elements of a sociology of racism by resolutely refusing to see race as an explanatory principle of social relations.

The author of *Democracy in America* not only confronted the question of the blacks in that country; he was also *rapporteur* in the Chamber of Deputies for a bill of 1839 on the abolition of slavery and the author of several reports on Algeria. As a political analyst, his first concern, so far as the USA was concerned, was to ask what would be the consequences of emancipating the blacks. The problem for him was not one of supposedly biological differences; he did not doubt the ability of black people to achieve a high level of civilization, given favourable conditions. The problem, for him, was social and political. Either, he suggested, the blacks are given their freedom and the whites merge with them, or slavery is maintained for as long as possible. 'Any intermediate measures seem to me likely to terminate, and that shortly,' he wrote, 'in the most horrible of civil wars, and perhaps in the extermination of one or other of the two races.'[19]

There is a real continuity between Tocqueville's analyses of the 'negro question' in the USA and of French colonization in Algeria. That continuity is characterized by a genuine tension between two perspectives, the ethical and the political, a tension which was not entirely resolved and which has been well described by Todorov. From the ethical point of view, Tocqueville condemns slavery and is also hostile to colonialism. But political realism and also, perhaps, where Algeria is concerned, a certain French nationalism dictate other attitudes: 'Slavery', he explains, writing of America (though, reading him, one cannot help thinking of the difficulties South Africa is experiencing today in its efforts to put apartheid behind it),

> is limited to one point on the globe and attacked by Christianity as unjust and by political economy as fatal; slavery, amid the democratic liberty and enlightenment of our age, is not an institution that can last. Either the slave or the master will put an end to it. In either case great misfortunes are to be anticipated.[20]

Tocqueville did not really decide firmly one way or the other between slavery and American democracy or between colonialism and the French nation's place in the world. On the other hand, he did decisively reject the 'false and odious doctrines' of racism which sought to legitimize the enslavement of the blacks on the grounds of their nature, rejected the idea of a racial influence on human behaviour and was highly critical of Gobineau, whose *Essai sur l'inégalité des races humaines* read, to him, like the 'Stud Book'.

But looking beyond these positions, which we would today describe as non-racist or anti-racist, the main point is that, without a shadow of a doubt, Tocqueville offers a genuine analysis of American anti-black racism. Admittedly, his reasoning only appears in outline, in a few, oft-quoted lines in which he points out that

> the white northerners shun Negroes with all the greater care, the more legislation has abolished any legal distinction between them. . . . In the North the white man afraid of mingling with the black is frightened by an imaginary danger. In the South, where the danger would be real, I do not think the fear would be less.[21]

We have here the guiding thread of an approach to the racism displayed by 'poor whites' fearing for the maintenance of their social position, an approach which will later be extensively developed, particularly in the work of Gunnar Myrdal.

Max Weber's contribution also develops out of a rejection of racist arguments, as presented by the biologists. He unhesitatingly attacks Chamberlain, shows concern at the rise of anti-semitism in Germany and, at the first National Congress of German Sociologists in 1910, puts up spirited opposition to the arguments of Dr Ploetz, the founder of *Rassenhygiene*, who regarded the flourishing of the social order as a flourishing of the race.[22] Weber proposes an analysis of 'poor white' racism which is akin to Tocqueville's:

> The 'poor white trash,' i.e., the propertyless and, in the absence of job opportunities, very often destitute white inhabitants of the southern states of the United States of America in the period of slavery, were the actual bearers of racial antipathy, which was quite foreign to the planters. This was so because the social honor of the 'poor whites' was dependent upon the social *déclassement* of the Negroes.[23]

But, first and foremost, Max Weber puts us on the path – which we shall explore much later in this work – of a link between community and what he calls 'race identity':

> A much more problematic source of social action than the sources analyzed above is 'race identity': common inherited traits that actually derive from common descent. Of course, race creates a 'group' only when it is subjectively perceived as a common trait: this happens only when a neighborhood or the mere proximity of racially different persons is the basis of joint (mostly political) action, or conversely, when some common experiences of members of the same race are linked to some antagonism against members of an *obviously* different group.[24]

For Max Weber, there is race only if there is a race consciousness, anchored in a communal identity, which can lead to action, such as segregation or contempt, for example, or, conversely, to fear of the other kind – 'antipathy is the primary and normal reaction'. And race conscious-ness is not attributable to hereditary differences but to a *habitus*: abhor-rence of sexual relations between races in the United States is 'socially determined'.[25] If, as John Gabriel and Gideon Ben-Tovim have shown, Weber does not deny the existence of biological differences between races, if at times he sees these as a factor which might contribute to the formation of ethnic groups, he none the less reverses pre-sociological reasoning by proposing to replace the concept of race by that of ethnic relations in which the sense of belonging to a race – and not necessarily the objective reality of race – contributes to orienting action.[26]

Tocqueville and Weber show us, then, each in his own way, that there can only be a sociological analysis of racism when the anti-sociological thinking which conflates the social and the biological – and subordinates the former to the latter – is rejected.[27] Both use the same term, too – that of 'race'. From these two points of view, they herald the first wave of genuine sociological research into 'race relations', which was to have its centre of excellence, from the 1920s onwards, in the Chicago School. But, before it could provide the first concrete data on race relations, that school of thought was to be preceded, both in the USA and in Europe, by a long period in which social thinking was dominated by biological notions.

3. Social thought and race in the United States

If we can profitably turn now to the United States, this is mainly because the contribution of American sociologists, in the broad sense, to the invention of racism was made under different conditions from those which can be seen to obtain in Europe. The major fact here is the presence of a large black population, reduced to slavery in the southern states until the Civil War, then subjected to a segregation which still largely continues today. The first two sociological treatises published in the USA in 1854 both undertook to justify the system of slavery: Henry Hughes's book stressing the moral and civic values of that system and George Fitzhugh's work adding to that perspective a call for an authoritarian order and Christian discipline.[28] It must be said that, in this period, writers in the North, 'generally uninformed and doctrinal, had little interest in research findings and objective realities, except as these could be used in the political controversy; the southern social students . . . were occupied in elaborating rationalizations of the institution of slavery'.[29] And it was to be one of the functions of important sectors of the emergent social sciences for a long time thereafter to legitimate the 'everyday' discourse most hostile to the egalitarian treatment of whites and blacks by providing a scientific version of that discourse. Among the most notable works in this regard were: Odum's *Social and Mental Traits of the Negro* of 1910, which reproduced all the popular prejudices relating to black people and developed the argument that they were incapable of assimilating; Ellwood's *Sociology and Modern Social Problems*, which spoke of the inferiority of the negro while suggesting that the superior race should give assistance to the inferior one; and the writings of Grove S. Dow, who called for a gradual segregation which would lead to the blacks being established in a single state.[30] A number of articles, even in the most prestigious journals – including the *American Journal of Sociology* – also developed an anti-black racism more akin to everyday thinking than to sociological analysis.

A second element characteristic of American thinking in the social sciences related not to the 'negro question' but, from the end of the nineteenth century and, particularly, from the First World War onwards, to the issue of immigration. The new arrivals caused the older population concern, giving rise to political debates which were themselves translated not just into immigration policies but also into a discourse with scientific pretensions. From that point on, deeply serious works described the – allegedly above-average – criminality of the newcomers and developed the idea that recent immigrants, and candidates for immigration, were characterized by racial differences which made it difficult and, in reality, undesirable, to assimilate them.[31]

Lastly, above and beyond the specific themes of the blacks and immigration, the European movement of racist thinking shaped the American social sciences at an early stage, and most analysts regard these as being dominated, at the turn of the century, by biological concepts.[32] Thus, for example, at least until 1910, one finds in the *American Journal of Sociology* articles by Galton, a translation of the introductory chapter of Vacher de Lapouge's work, *L'Aryen*, and several articles by American authors directly inspired by their European counterparts. And writers whose thinking was specifically racist, like Madison Grant and Lothrop Stoddard, also enjoyed considerable success.[33]

As in Europe, important figures in social thinking in the USA resisted racial doctrines and theories. Lester Ward firmly rejected Galton's theses; William G. Sumner called for an end to attributing to race what in fact pertained to the mores and the ethos of a people; Charles H. Cooley introduced the notion of caste, thereby opening the way for what would be a genuine mode of analysis of race relations.[34] More precisely, the first two decades of the twentieth century saw sketched out the two major orientations of what would become the first sociological approach to racism – on the one hand, the theme of castes and racial prejudice and, on the other, that of concrete relations between races. Here again, as in Tocqueville and Weber, we see that the transition to a sociological position, though it means a move towards investigating racism rather than explaining social functioning and historical evolution in terms of race, nevertheless does not eliminate this latter notion. Thus, both in Europe and in the USA, social thinking extricated itself only late in the day, partially and with difficulty, from racist doctrines which, indeed, it often formulated and disseminated. In the 1920s, however, the social sciences did clearly begin to make the change which led from explanation in terms of race to the analysis of racism.

2

RACE RELATIONS

If we now have to turn, much more even than in the preceding chapter, towards American sociology, this is because it was responsible for the first move towards – and most important expression of – the change in thinking which cleared the way for the concrete analysis of racism. Two central ideas governed the way this change was expressed. On the one hand, there was a tendency to shift the frame of reference from race to culture, though this did not stop writers continuing to use the term 'race' at every turn. On the other hand, the focus was no longer on innate or acquired features characterizing a particular human group, but on – predominantly inter-cultural – relations between groups. What developed in the USA in the twentieth century, first in rudimentary form, then with greater precision in the 1920s – after blacks had served in the American ranks in the First World War and, particularly, when they began to move in large numbers into the great northern industrial cities – was a sociology of 'race relations'. From that point on, the aim was to make a concrete study of social and inter-cultural realities concerning, among other things, relations between whites and blacks within a society which, as early as that period, was reluctant to see itself as a melting pot, to the point, indeed, of excluding blacks from its self-image.[1]

Many thinkers laid the ground for this. W.E.B. Du Bois, both as an analyst of, and as a campaigner in, the black cause, published his famous study of 'negroes' in Philadelphia as early as 1899, and, subsequently, produced many works which particularly strove to give American blacks a history, a culture and a role in the construction of American democracy.[2] The importance of notions like mores, ethos or culture, for example, owes much to a sociologist like Sumner, and also to the birth of a cultural anthropology which, with Franz Boas and his school, breaks with physical anthropology and moves towards a cultural relativism which involves a clean break with all forms of racist prejudice: in 1911, Franz Boas closed the first Universal Congress on Race with the assertion that the 'old idea' of the absolute stability of human types must in all evidence be rejected and, with it, 'belief in the hereditary superiority' of certain types over others.[3] Reflecting to a greater or lesser extent the influence of Darwinism and the arguments of Ludwig Gumplowicz and Gustav Ratzenhofer, a style of thinking in terms of 'race struggle' had also gained adherents and, when such thinking rid itself of racism and any notion of the biological superiority of one race over another, it informed the analysis of conflict between human groups, as, for example, in the work of Lester F. Ward.[4] Lastly, another notion began to be widely used in the description of segregation: that of caste. This had mainly been developed, as we have already mentioned, by Charles H. Cooley, and was the basic concept used by a great number of writers to analyse the American racial structure until it was fiercely criticized, as we shall see, by Oliver Cox.[5]

The major figure, however, from the point of view which concerns us here, was undoubtedly Robert E. Park, founder, with Ernest Burgess, of the so-called 'Chicago school'. He joined the faculty of that city's university in 1913 after first working as a journalist, studying in Europe and acting as secretary to Booker T. Washington, a campaigner for black rights in the southern states of the USA.

There are a great many indications throughout Park's work of his constant interest in the theme of 'race relations', and also modifications – sometimes significant ones – of the categories by which it was to be analysed.[6] We shall not examine these transformations here since our object is not so much to construct a systematic history of ideas as to bring out nodal moments or styles of thinking in which new paradigms, new approaches are forged. For this reason, we shall content ourselves for the moment with highlighting what seem to us the most crucial aspects of the work of Robert E. Park.

1. An evolutionistic optimism

Like so many other intellectuals of his time, Robert E. Park developed an evolutionistic style of thinking which set the emergence of race relations within a broad historical perspective. In his view, race relations are a part of the modern world; they arose as a consequence of Europe reaching out, first commercially, then in its politics and religion, to the rest of the world, before bringing industry and capitalism to that world and, most importantly, causing great upheavals among its populations. Those relations should in the end become smoother as modernity became established and as differences came to be based less on race and inheritance and increasingly on culture and work: 'race conflicts in the modern world, which is already or presently will be a single great society, will be more and more in the future confused with, and eventually superseded by, the conflicts of classes'.[7]

This global evolutionist perspective can also be seen in the more limited analysis Park offers of race relations in the USA. In the beginning, he explains, there were no race problems, no social relations between whites and blacks because the latter were slaves and excluded from the field of social competition. Slavery was then followed by a caste system, which also ruled out the idea of a relation. At that point a social order prevailed in which relations between racial groups or peoples of different colour were strictly regulated by an 'etiquette', as the title of a book by Bertram W. Doyle, on which Park commented in glowing terms, asserted.[8] Etiquette, explained Park, is the very essence of a caste system, a set of rituals, a kind of social arrangement in which everyone does what is expected of him without forfeiting his inner freedom. With the caste system, as with slavery, the race problem had found its 'natural solution'. Each race had a monopoly of its own tasks and 'when this status is accepted by the subject people, as is the case where the caste or slavery systems become fully established, racial competition ceases and racial animosity tends to disappear'. Each race is in its place and 'no obstacle to racial cooperation exists'.[9]

But the caste system had begun to break down and blacks were affected by all kinds of change. Many had left the rural south for the urban, industrial north; a black middle class was forming, along with a black intelligentsia; the level of education of the blacks had risen and the United States had entered the era of race relations. The black problem became the problem of a democratic and liberal society which set a premium on individual competition and where each person had the same theoretical opportunities for upward mobility, but where it was tempting for those already in the race – the whites – to restrict the access of those who were not yet in it, but threatening to join it – namely, the blacks. From this point of view, racial prejudice has an instrumental function: it serves to prevent – or restrain – blacks from becoming competitive.

In Park's view, this 'race relations' phase should not itself last forever. Just as individualism and democracy had done away first with slavery, then with caste distinctions, racial distinctions should in future fade and be forgotten and ignored. They represented a last phase in the forward march of modernity before social groups came to define themselves in truly social terms – the last resistance of the Old World, a phenomenon of the transition from 'ascription' to 'achievement'. For the moment, however, American society was right in the middle of that transition and it was proper, therefore, to engage in very concrete study of race relations between whites and blacks and to undertake applied research. Park himself set an example in this regard, exerting a central, direct influence on the work of the Chicago Commission on Race Relations, set up after the race riots which, between 27 July and 8 August 1919, left 38 dead (33 of them black) and 537 injured (342 blacks).[10]

2. Race relations and race consciousness

According to Park, race relations are the relations which exist 'between peoples distinguished by marks of racial descent, particularly when these racial differences enter into the consciousness of the individuals and groups so distinguished, and by so doing determine in each case the individual's conception of himself as well as his status in the community'.[11] And everything which reinforces the physical visibility of the individual and, by that same token, his/her ethnic or genetic identity, also reinforces his/her 'race consciousness' and creates conditions favourable to race relations:

'race consciousness . . . is to be regarded as a phenomenon, like class or caste consciousness. . . . Race relations . . . are not so much the relations that exist between individuals of different races as between individuals conscious of these differences.'[12]

Such statements well illustrate the ambiguity of a style of thinking which aims to explain a relationship between races. On the one hand, these statements regard race both as an objective and a subjective reality, and thus may veer off fairly directly into racism. This is indeed the criticism which Joyce A. Ladner makes of Park in a work of 1973 which presents itself to some extent as the manifesto of black American sociology.[13] On the other hand, Park's assertions may serve as a basis for an applied sociology, for the kind of fieldwork which Park proposed to conduct on four distinct, hierarchically structured, but interdependent levels: the ecological, the economic, the political and the personal and cultural.

It is principally on this basis that the study of race relations – by Park, but also by Burgess and many other writers after them – speaks of adaptation, colonization, invasion, isolation, migration, parasitism and segregation; that it describes four modes of interaction (competition, conflict, accommodation and assimilation); and that, with these kinds of categories, it sees itself as part of an urban ecology which constitutes the city as a physical unit within which the processes of spatial segregation and the mechanisms of adaptation to the environment on the part of each of the groups in question can be observed. Everett C. Hughes, another member of the Chicago School, defined this urban ecology project well: the aim was to study 'contacts of peoples and the situations in which such contacts occur' and, in so doing, to avoid the ethnocentric point of view which focusses on one group, such as an ethnic minority: 'the true unit of race and ethnic relations is not the single ethnic group, but the *situation*, embracing all of the diverse groups who live in the community or region.'[14] He was particularly interested in the sites of contact itself, the racial and cultural *frontiers* and, by 'ecology of ethnic or racial contact', he meant 'the processes which determine the relative number, the spatial distribution, and the division of labor between peoples: what they do for and to one another that affects their survival, and their economic behavior'.[15]

More generally, the perspective opened up by Park set the tone of, and still dominates, an immense research field in which very empirical studies are made of the phenomena of racial, social and spatial segregation, of the functioning of ethnic or racial minorities – both internally and in their relations with other groups – and of the transformations of the city which all this generates and sustains. In a sense, by according importance to empirical data and observation in the field, the study of race relations has opened the way for the analysis of certain elementary forms of racism: concrete behaviours, whether they be of violence, discrimination or segregation. Its strength has been that it has moved away from the study of characteristics specific to races or ethnic groups, as it defines them, to analyse very real phenomena: physical, geographical, territorial, economic and cultural contacts and conflicts. Its main weakness, contrary to what has often been asserted, lies not so much in a certain naturalism – based chiefly on the idea of an ecological cycle (conflict, accommodation, assimilation) which, as Park observed, 'does not proceed with the same ease and the same speed in all cases',[16] – as in the idea that there is a direct link between racist prejudice and a dominant position in a race-relations situation.

Racism, even though, as we should recall, the expression is anachronistic in this context, is primarily for Park an expression of 'conservatism', a 'resistance of the social order to change'.[17] This is a rather summary explanation of racist prejudice. In particular, by not questioning the notion of race, chiefly in what it claims as its objective aspects, Park and his closest followers based their sociology on a category, while under-estimating that that category was to a great extent a social and historical construct; they were unaware of, or under-estimated, the mechanisms which produced racism in all those cases where it was based not necessarily on concrete relations or lived experience but, much rather, on representations and fantasies, on an imaginary register which does not always bear much relation to the objective characteristics to which it purports to refer. The race relations school has garnered concrete knowledge and enabled us to distance ourselves – though not entirely – from biological theories of race. It treated these as an element in the identity of communal actors much more than really concerning itself with racism.[18]

3. Race, caste and class

'Originally,' explains Park,

> race relations in the South could be rather accurately represented by a horizontal line, with all the white folk above and all the Negro folk below. . . . With the development of industrial and professional classes within the Negro race, the distinction between the races tends to assume the form of a vertical line. On one side of this line the Negro is represented in most of the occupational and professional classes; on the other side of the line the white man is similarly represented. . . . The result is to develop in every occupational class professional and industrial bi-racial organizations. Bi-racial organizations preserve race distinction, but change their content.[19]

This idea of a double distinction on the basis of class – that is, of relative position in the scale of social stratification – and on the basis of caste – that is, of segregation fixed by a 'colour line' – enables the sociology of race relations to escape being confined purely to an urban or spatial ecology and allows it to concern itself with the general structure of – in this case, American – society. This idea was given precise formulation by W. Lloyd Warner, who, in a text which is well summed up by the famous diagram he proposed (see Figure 2.1), turned Park's line into a diagonal one.[20]

This diagram and the key idea underlying it have often been discussed and criticized, by W.E.B. Du Bois, Gunnar Myrdal, Oliver Cox and many other researchers.[21] It seems to us that the attempt to link the notions of race, class and caste in this way produces an empirical representation of the

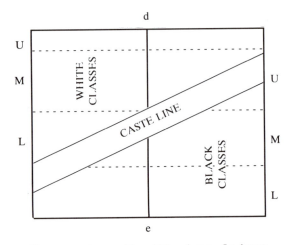

U: upper classes; M: middle classes; L: lower
classes; de: last position of caste line

Figure 2.1

place of blacks in American society rather than any kind of theory of
racism. It operates on the basis of a 'weak' definition of the notion of class,
which is in fact synonymous with social status,[22] and a questionable use of
the notion of caste, imported from India, possibly via the work of Max
Weber, without any great effort of critical reflexion. It is of interest,
however, for having initiated the work of what are today very important
currents of thinking which study the operation of the social system in terms
of its mechanisms of rejection and exclusion, mechanisms in which racism
properly so called *combines* with the marginalization of a proletariat or
sub-proletariat, and racial oppression with economic and social subordination.[23] We shall see below how we have to move from the 'colour line',
still rooted as yet in the idea of caste, to the notion of racism, or from
notions of status or class, as used by Warner, to the concept of social
movement. For the moment, however, we can take it that an important
advance had been made here, one which not only made available certain
analytical tools, however ambiguous these might appear to us today, but
also inspired research work in the field, such as the long and insightful
participant observation study by John Dollard in a small town in the
deepest South or, in the same vein of 'community studies', the study of the
Deep South carried out by W. Lloyd Warner in the town of Natchez on the
Mississippi.[24] And this advance itself is the more substantial in that it
brings us immediately, through Dollard's work in particular, to an entirely
new perspective in which racism appears as a set of prejudices and
attitudes, an 'emotional structure', and not merely as a by-product or
instrumental rationalization of a situation in which one race is dominated
by another.

3
PREJUDICE AND PERSONALITY

The study of race relations, the contribution – and, also, the limitations – of which we have just examined, constitutes, in Michael Banton's phrase, a 'proto-sociology' of racism; a second shift of focus, which occurs largely within that field, will take us much more distinctly into the analysis of racism and, more precisely, of one of its basic forms, prejudice.

Here again, the most important testing ground, if not for ideas then at least for concrete research, has been the USA.

1. From race relations to theories of prejudice

The transition which occurs towards the end of the 1930s from the sociology of race relations to that of racist prejudice is nowhere so evident as in John Dollard's study of 'Southerntown', to which reference has already been made. This is the fictive name given to the town in the south of the USA where Dollard, a white researcher from the north, lived for many months, in order to study *in situ* how economic, political and personal life were shaped by a caste system. The wealth of Dollard's observations is impressive and what he writes of the researcher's relationship with the object of his research is also worthy of study. However, we are chiefly concerned with his book here for the theory of prejudice which forms its conclusion.

Like many other writers before him, Dollard saw prejudice as being rooted in a situation, in a relationship between races. It represented 'a defensive attitude intended to preserve white prerogatives in the caste situation and aggressively to resist any pressure from the Negro side to change his inferior position'.[1] But it could not be explained by the lived reality of that situation, by the concrete relationship between blacks and whites. It had to be analysed on its own terms and that analysis required psycho-sociological categories which themselves owe much to debates on the relationship between culture and personality current at the time of writing, and also to the influence of Freud. Dollard, Daniel Patrick Moynihan reminds us in his preface to the 1988 edition of *Caste and Class in a Southern Town*, was the 'first Freudian' in American social science.[2]

The decisive idea here is perhaps better formulated by Eugene L. Horowitz, a psychologist whom Dollard cites at length, than by himself: 'attitudes toward Negroes are now chiefly determined not by contact with Negroes, but by contact with the prevalent attitude toward Negroes.'[3]

Prejudice reproduces itself, and we understand that reproduction the better because we possess a psycho-social theory of aggression and frustration; we have to turn our attention, therefore, to the bearers of racial prejudice, their personality formation and the way they cope with their personal and collective difficulties. In every individual, explains Dollard, the restrictions experienced during childhood and the problems of adult life give rise to frustrations and, in response or reaction to these frustrations, to aggression or hostility. But hostility cannot be expressed within one's own group, which discourages its being shown, and it will therefore find an outlet elsewhere, particularly where a tradition of racial prejudice permits this: 'Race prejudice is mysterious because no real occasion is required for its expression; the object does not necessarily have to offend or frustrate. On the contrary there are deflected to the object against which one is prejudiced the hostilities that should be directed toward nearer and dearer persons.'[4] According to Dollard, three 'key concepts' can shed light on racial prejudice:

- that of generalized or 'free-floating' aggression, which is itself linked to the frustrations of the whites;
- that of a permissive social pattern where racism is concerned, which makes it possible to isolate a detested, defenceless group within society, against whom hostility will be directed;
- lastly, the object must be uniformly identifiable, which means that it is possible easily to recognize those whom it is normal to dislike.

This theorization is not far removed from the idea of 'scapegoating' and there is much that could be said in criticism of it. It is, in particular, difficult to see how it could apply to situations in which the Other – most obviously, the Jew – is hated all the more for being, in actual fact, not visible or identifiable, and where not merely race, but also physical characteristics are a totally imaginary construction. But the essential point is that, with Dollard, the analysis ceases to centre on a relationship between the races and the emphasis begins to shift markedly towards the racist actor. Prejudice is no longer the instrumental rationalization of a domination, or, at least, it is no longer merely that. It becomes, rather, a mode of resolving problems and tensions which have their origin elsewhere than in contact between races: namely, in the lived experience of the members of the racializing group, who find in the racialized group an outlet for their social and psychological difficulties.

2. The American dilemma

This perspective was considerably broadened – as were others -with the appearance of the positively monumental work that is Gunnar Myrdal's *American Dilemma. The Negro Problem and Modern Democracy*.[5] It would be absurd and contrary to our objectives here to attempt to provide an exhaustive account of this vast edifice at which an impressive number of researchers laboured over four years. We shall content ourselves once again with pointing up a number of the advances made, beginning with those which allow us clearly to mark the break with earlier approaches. The tone is, in fact, set by Myrdal in the Introduction to his book: the 'Negro problem' in the USA 'is a problem in the heart of the American';[6] it is a moral question, a dilemma, which is chiefly the concern of the whites, who live out an internal conflict between, on the one hand, the 'American *creed*' – a set of high national and Christian precepts, and moral values – and, on the other, the valorization of individual or specific economic, social and sexual interests, of considerations of prestige and conformity, in short, of individualistic orientations which find expression in oppression of the blacks. This is why, explains Myrdal, his book is concerned primarily with what goes on in the minds of the whites. At the outset, he had thought he had to put the accent on the black population and its characteristics: manner of life, feelings, social stratification, migration, religion, delin-quency, etc. Gradually, however, it became 'increasingly evident that little, if anything, could be scientifically explained in terms of the peculiarities of the Negroes themselves':[7] the concept of the 'Negro' is a social, not a biological one, and racism is based not on knowledge of the Other, but, much rather, on ignorance. Ignorance, for Myrdal, does not imply lack of interest or curiosity. It is, rather, a more or less necessary restriction which gives rise to stereotypes and magic formulas that are always laden with emotion; knowledge is constantly twisted in one direction – 'toward classifying the Negro low and the white high'.[8] Ignorance is also a way of referring to the blacks impersonally – 'them', 'they' – or of only speaking negatively of them – about their crimes, for example. Ignorance is virtually tantamount to avoidance or negation of the black problem, with the result that the picture of a black person is seldom printed in the press in the southern states of the USA. The black person is indeed, to use Ralph Ellison's famous phrase, the 'invisible man'.[9]

Myrdal is also struck by the irrational character of racism: the same Southerner, for example, will sing the praises of the 'good old Negroes' and denounce the vices of the young ones, who are recalcitrant and corrupted by schooling, at the same time as bemoaning the ignorance and backwardness of the former and enthusing over the intelligence and progressiveness he sees in the latter.

Lastly, racism keeps the blacks in an inferior social position and, from this point of view, chiefly involves those who are most afraid of seeing the distance between themselves and the blacks disappear, that is, the 'poor whites', who are often close to the blacks socially and who take out on them the discrimination, threats, exploitation and frustrations they them-selves experience in their social relations with other whites. This argument is taken much further by Myrdal than it was in Tocqueville or Weber, where we have already seen it outlined. It includes an explanation of the lesser racism observable among the white upper classes, who, thanks to the care taken by the 'poor whites' to mark a racial distance, are relieved of this 'otherwise painful task, necessary to the monopolization of the power and the advantages'.[10] He also suggests that racist ideology allows whites from different social backgrounds, who, in other circumstances, would be opposed to, or would keep apart from, one another, to come together. This idea, though well documented, was to be vigorously contested by a whole series of writers of a Marxist or near-Marxist persuasion, beginning with Oliver Cox, who draws on the very different image of a community of interests between proletarians white and black. Since it ensures the maintenance of a distance which is, socially, in danger of disappearing, racism cannot tolerate racial intermixing and thus takes the form of sanctions – even lethal sanctions (lynchings) – whenever the purity of the race is threatened from the white point of view. Illicit relations between a white man and a black woman are possible – and described by Myrdal – but not the opposite, and, above all, racial intermixing is an obsessive fear and the marriage of a white woman to a black man is intolerable. The refusal of social equality, segregation and discrimination in all spheres of life – in leisure activities, at church, in education, politics, housing or employment – might almost be understood, ultimately, as a precaution to prevent biological intermixing – a thesis not far removed from the argument which stresses the desire for physical homofiliation as an explanation of the ultimate foundations of racism.[11]

Myrdal's central idea, that of a dilemma between, on the one hand, the highest values of the American nation and its democracy and, on the other, the tendency to exclude blacks from these things does not mean that he regards the situation as frozen. He believes, in fact, that progress is possible and can indeed be observed taking place, in the form of the individual assimilation of blacks and, most importantly, in changes in the mentality of the whites.[12] Myrdal has been criticized for being blind to the forms of organization of American blacks, which were not in fact to develop, in the main, until the 1960s; for underestimating the less positive, less idealistic elements of the 'American creed'; and for speaking of a 'dilemma' where it would have been better to speak of incoherence.[13] He has also been accused of refusing to see the material situation of blacks and adopting, in Cox's words, a 'mystical' approach.

Such criticisms should not, however, cause us to lose sight of the impressive range of data and analyses assembled by Myrdal. Above all, they should not be allowed to mask the chief virtue of his reasoning, which is an acceptance that, in order to understand racism, one should turn aside from the concrete experience of the relations between blacks and whites – though this is, in fact, also covered to a considerable extent – and give priority to examining the ideological work carried out by whites on themselves, to looking at their internal contradictions, their dilemmas.

3. Racism and personality

Neither Dollard nor Myrdal, to confine ourselves to these two major figures, breaks totally with empirical observation of race relations, observation 'in the field'. They are detached, but in no sense disengaged from the social realities within which racism unfolds. Others, however, will go much further, freeing themselves yet more from the situation in which racism can be observed to examine its psycho-social bases and to see in these, first and foremost, the expression of a personality type.

We ought, perhaps, to turn at this point to such important authors as Eysenck, Allport or Klineberg.[14] Yet the decisive step was taken, in the clearest possible way, by researchers who, though they worked in the United States, fundamentally defined their position by reference to an experience which had occurred elsewhere, though some of them had lived through it: the experience of Nazi anti-semitism and the so-called 'final solution' in Europe. Could a link be found between the expression of prejudice and personality traits? Were there individual predispositions to prejudice and, if so, what did they consist in? What made someone receptive, or not, to a speech by Goebbels? These were the questions, formulated by Max Horkheimer, which inspired the study programme on prejudice sponsored by the American Jewish Committee. Within that programme a number of writers were to strive to show how an intense experience could reinforce the links between personality and prejudice. It was in the light of these considerations that Bruno Bettelheim and Morris Janowitz were to study ethnic intolerance among soldiers who had undergone great privations, but had also enjoyed the prestige of being Second World War fighters, and were subsequently experiencing a sense of downward social mobility. In this light too that Leo Lowenthal and Norbert Guterman concerned themselves with the mechanisms whereby a diffuse emotion became transformed into political conviction and action.[15]

Within this research programme, shaped by a fear of seeing a Nazi-type phenomenon reproduced and a concern to contribute to the root-and-branch eradication of racism at the point where the personality is formed, the work which most merits our interest is indisputably the famous study of the authoritarian personality carried out under Adorno's direction.[16]

Adorno's central hypothesis is that an individual's convictions, whether economic, social or political, form a relatively broad and coherent pattern, as if bound together by a 'mentality' or a 'spirit'. For Adorno, this pattern is an expression of deep-lying trends in the personality.

This latter is formed in childhood, particularly within the family and by upbringing, but is not given once and for all: it 'is a product of the social environment'.[17] Racism, or, more precisely, anti-semitism – which is the object of Adorno's research – is related to a particular personality type, which is authoritarian, anti-democratic, conservative, politically right-wing and informed by a highly ethnocentric ideology. The authoritarian personality is more common among persons professing religious affiliations, particularly when the acceptance of religion expresses submission to a clear-cut model of parental authority; it implies little genuine love for the parents, a stereotyped, superficial glorification laden with resentment and a sense of victimization at their hands. The feeling of admiration is accepted, but the underlying hostility is repressed. The authoritarian personality minimizes parental conflicts and reproduces the family discipline known in childhood, where it was experienced as arbitrary. The mix of superficial identification with the parents on the part of the child and resentment towards them, and towards authority in general, finds expression in a phenomenon of overconformity, accompanied by a desire simultaneously to destroy established authority, traditions and institutions, an ambivalence that was at the heart of Nazism and which also shows itself with regard to sexual matters (surface admiration, but underlying resentment, of the opposite sex). Lastly, the authoritarian personality is very conformist and shows little capacity to recognize – and hence to manage – its own impulsive tendencies or to express its fear, weakness and sexuality, which leads to threat, weakness, etc., being externalized on to others.

The methods employed by Adorno are as far removed as can be from those applied in participant observation or empirical field studies of 'race relations'. The aim here, going beyond factual questions, is to locate individuals on opinion or attitude scales and identify in each of them, with the aid of projective techniques, the possible signs of an authoritarian personality structure. Thus, after having conducted a survey of more than 2,000 people with the aid of a questionnaire (members of clubs, patients in psychiatric hospitals, prison inmates, students at a school for merchant marine officers, men and women from various social milieus), those who achieved the highest (top 25 per cent) and the lowest (bottom 25 per cent) scores on the ethnocentrism scale drawn up by Adorno were studied in greater depth, the aim being to delve more thoroughly into their personalities.

This research, which showed up the presence in the United States of distinctly authoritarian types with anti-semitic tendencies, made a considerable impact and prompted many other studies in the same vein, together with copious criticism, which was sometimes very constructive, as in the case of Milton Rokeach's comments.[18] The important point here is to stress the shift brought about by the conceptual framework adopted by Adorno. Racism is presented in this work as originating outside the situation in which it may possibly be expressed; it relates to something quasi-invariant – personality factors – even if it only appears openly in a favourable context. Rather like Sartre, whose 'Portrait of the Anti-Semite'[19] he only discovered when his own research was coming to an end, and to whom he says he felt very close at that point, Adorno sees anti-semites as individuals who, given their personalities, react in a particular way in given situations: 'the forces of personality are not responses but *readinesses for response*'.[20] For Adorno, racial prejudice is no longer a more or less rational instrumentalization of a domination, nor even, as in the work of Myrdal, a moral problem, one of the terms of a contradiction lived out by a dominant group; it is rooted in the depths of the psyche. We are not yet in a pure anthropology or psychology of racism here since, in Adorno, the authoritarian personality is the product of a process of socialization and education. But we are coming close to it, in increasingly specifying a hard core of the phenomenon external to the concrete social relations within which it is manifested – something, incidentally, which we might regard as surprising on the part of a man who was one of the leading figures of the Frankfurt School and who is some considerable way here from Marxism as reinterpreted by that school.

4. The fragmentation of the object

With Adorno, who calls for two types of factors to be distinguished in anti-semitism – on the one hand, situational factors and, on the other, factors of personality – a dissociation between two orders of problem becomes clear: those relating to the social system and those having to do with the racist actor. At the same time, race and racism, for this author as for many others, are totally separated; racism is to be explained independently of a reference to any presumed reality of race – something which Sartre also says, in his way, in a celebrated formula when he asserts that the Jew is defined by the gaze of the Other: 'it is the anti-Semite who creates the Jew'.[21]

This considerable development in the thinking on this subject prompts us to make three observations. The first concerns the more widespread occurrence – though this development predates Adorno's study – of work centred on the psychology of racism and racial prejudice, which, as Allport explains, is distinguished from prejudgement insofar as a prejudice is 'not reversible when exposed to new knowledge' and actively resists the evidence that would unseat it.[22] Racism, particularly in a psychoanalytic perspective, comes to be seen as the incapacity of some people to manage difference, but also their incapacity to cope with the resemblance with the Other, the foreigner and, also, women. And that incapacity, which is differently expressed depending on the circumstances, or indeed the social milieu, is inscribed in an unconscious which the analyst is regarded as the person best placed to unveil. Thus, in an interview with the biologist Albert Jacquard, J.-B. Pontalis observes that what is primary is the dread the Other inspires. But

> that dread is a fascination and thus also an attraction. . . . That foreigner [*étranger*] is not just any old foreigner. He only provokes a sense of foreignness because he is also my fellow [*semblable*]. . . . This is why I regard as false, or at least incomplete, the accepted idea that racism represents a radical rejection of the Other, a deep-seated intolerance of difference, etc. Contrary to what is normally thought, the image of one's fellow, of the *double*, is infinitely more disturbing than the image of the Other.[23]

For her part, Julia Kristeva goes even further: the Other, the alien producing animosity and irritation, is in fact my own unconscious, the return of the repressed or, to be quite precise, of the fear of death and, also, for men, of the female sex: 'the foreigner is within us'[24] and, 'when we flee from or struggle against the foreigner, we are fighting our unconscious'. Here, racism no longer has anything to do with race, nor even with the characteristics of those against whom it is targeted; it is naturalized, lurking deep in the unconscious or identified with that unconscious in what tends to be a de-socializing perspective.

This point of view is based on the idea that the notion of human races is itself meaningless. That notion, still current among those working on 'race relations', has long been rejected, except within certain minority tendencies, whose importance should not be under-estimated, where measurement of bones and observation of skin pigmentation has given way to the study of genes. However, the decline of the notion of race was never so sharp – and this is our second observation – as after the Second World War and the discovery of Auschwitz, when UNESCO embarked upon the scientific denunciation of racist doctrines and a great many scientists – the most eminent biologists among them – explained that the idea of race was a nonsense and that the genetic distance between individuals of the same 'race', for example, is comparable to that between two supposed races.[25]

Lastly – our third observation – it is clear that, at the point when it was being abandoned by the majority of scientific and moral authorities in the Western world, the idea of race paradoxically began to make ground among those whom it had previously stigmatized, oppressed or excluded. This was at times a surprising product of a cultural relativism pushed to extremes. Thus, in 1947, at the instigation of Melville Herskovits, the American Anthropological Association filed a petitition with the United Nations Organization for a declaration on human rights aimed at outlawing racial and cultural discrimination. Herskovits's position, which set off a serious controversy, was based on the idea that the black communities in the New World drew sustenance from the surviving elements of their original African cultures which had withstood uprooting to America, the experience of slavery and its abolition. This implied that there was, among American blacks, an irreducible core related to their origins, which made assimilation impossible. However, the most spectacular phenomenon in this connection relates not to intellectual arguments of this kind, but to the development, against the backdrop of an upsurge of nationalism and anti-colonialist action, of identity-based movements oscillating between self-definitions that are predominantly cultural, historical and political and others which are chiefly racial, these latter, for example, involving appeals to African-ness or negritude, or the project of a 'Black Power'.

These three observations are interconnected. From the moment the conceptual framework of race relations breaks up, even if there is still some genuine life left in it today, thinking on this subject itself becomes fragmented, going off in at least the three directions we have just mentioned: race becomes an anti-scientific, harmful notion for those who speak in the name of science and morality; it is brandished in their struggle by dominated or excluded groups and their ideologues; whilst racism seems to detach itself from the lived experience of contact between groups defined by race to appear as a more or less de-socialized or naturalized attribute of individuals expressing a mentality or personality-type.[26] In a way, this allows us to define more precisely what is at issue in a sociology of racism. That sociology has everything to gain from jettisoning the notion of race as a category of analysis. But it has much to lose by moving away from the study of *relations*. In focussing on the racist actor, and the prejudices and personality of that actor, the social sciences are recognizing an essential dimension of the racist phenomenon – one which cannot be understood without reference to the consciousness or subjectivity of the actor. But they are running the risk of decontextualizing that consciousness or subjectivity, of disengaging racism from the relations within which it arises or develops. The difficulty of reducing these relations to race relations should not, however, lead us to dissociate the prejudiced individual or racist personality from the relations in which racism becomes established and is expressed, but should commit us to identify these social and inter-societal relations and examine the processes of management – and loss – of meaning to which racism gives expression. To sum up, the theories of prejudice and the personality invite us to study the actor; those of race relations remind us, even if they offer an unsatisfactory definition of the actor, that there is no actor without a system of action, without social or inter-societal relations.

4

RACISM AS IDEOLOGY

The horror inspired by Nazi anti-semitism, the debates around decoloniz-ation – when the peoples and nations of the Third World began to assert themselves as such – and the rise of the black movements in the USA in the 1960s, together with the smaller movements in the French and British West Indies, each in their way make it difficult to keep to analyses focussed wholly and solely on individuals defined in terms of prejudice or person-ality structure. Confronted with a racism which has taken on more or less institutional form within states or political forces and, in particular, with an anti-semitism which was at the very heart of the experience of the Third Reich, academic concern has also been directed towards political analyses of the phenomenon, perceived in this case as a major ideology or, at the very least, as a form of mythic thinking informing political action.

1. Racist ideology

Throughout the nineteenth century, within European societies, scientific racism was little more than a set of doctrines and opinions meeting with a relatively wide degree of public approval. When those doctrines and opinions entered the political arena, they became full-blown ideologies, that is, in the words of Hannah Arendt,

> systems based upon a single opinion that proved strong enough to attract and persuade a majority of people and broad enough to lead them through the various experiences and situations of an average modern life. For an ideology differs from a simple opinion in that it claims to possess either the key to history, or the solution for all the 'riddles of the universe', or the intimate knowledge of the hidden universal laws which are supposed to rule nature and man.[1]

With this definition, Arendt ranges racism among the great political problems of the twentieth century: 'Every full-fledged ideology has been created, continued and improved as a political weapon and not as a theoretical doctrine. . . [W]ithout immediate contact with political life none of them could be imagined.'[2]

Thus, in her major work on the origins of totalitarianism, Hannah Arendt devotes a whole chapter to the birth of racist ideology, a phenomenon she regards as profoundly modern and Western. Her approach not only has the merit of examining how racism made the transition to the political level, but also of showing how that process was effected in distinct ways in France, Britain and Germany, its three most important initial breeding grounds.

In France, the point of departure is to be found within a very precise social category, the nobility, which felt threatened even before the Revolution of 1789. In the early years of the eighteenth century, the Comte de Boulainvilliers was, if we accept Arendt's description, the precursor of a racism which had its origins in the fears of the aristocracy. He was not able to accept the identification of the King and the monarchy alone with the whole of the nation, but he was, also, conscious of the rise of the Third Estate. Thus, between King and people, he could not readily see a place for the nobility. For this reason, he claimed an original distinction for it, a specificity relating to its genealogical origins. He thus outlined a style of aristocratic racial thinking which enabled him to set the people and the bourgeoisie, on the one hand, against the absolute monarchy, on the other. After the Revolution, Gobineau, who was, in Hannah Arendt's words, 'a curious mixture of frustrated nobleman and romantic intellectual',[3] also drifted into a race thinking which reflected the decline of the nobility: 'Step by step, he identified the fall of his caste with the fall of France, then of Western civilization, then of the whole of mankind.'[4] Thus, in France, the birth of racism would be brought about by a social group, the nobility, which could do no other than oppose the French nation as invented by both of its adversaries, the monarchy and the Third Estate. In the beginning, then, French racism was relatively anti-patriotic and non-nationalistic, if not indeed pro-Germanic.

Things are completely different in the case of Germany, where the ground for race thinking was laid by the question of national unity. Both during and after the war of 1814, the German Romantics exalted the innate personality and natural nobility; and, since Germany had no political unity, the German nationalists proposed an ideological definition of the nation and spoke of a common tribal origin. These two currents long ran side by side and were, in each case, 'but temporary means of escape from political realities. Once welded together [at the end of the nineteenth century], they formed the very basis for racism as a full-fledged ideology.'[5]

Lastly, in Britain, racism also went together with nationalism. In the writings of Burke, for example, at the time of the French Revolution, one finds the idea that the British people or nation possessed a right to freedom as an entailed inheritance – the rights, not of man, but of Englishmen. This idea, which was very widespread, would later be complemented first by the doctrine of polygenism – which asserted an absolute distance between races, since they had various and distinct origins – then by Darwinism, which provided 'the ideological weapons for race as well as class rule' by explaining that only the fittest survive (the work of Darwinism here was later continued by eugenics). There are two important moments in this process, according to Hannah Arendt's analysis. First, racism was connected at a very early stage with British colonial expansion and, more precisely, with the project of empire-building. Here, Benjamin Disraeli is a central figure. That statesman did not think in terms of colonies, referring indeed to 'the colonial deadweight which we do not govern', but of empire.

He it was who implanted the British administration in India, ensuring, as Hannah Arendt puts it, 'the establishment of an exclusive caste in a foreign country whose only function was rule and not colonization'.[6] Now, Disraeli, not apparently trammelled by his Jewish origins, is typical of a racism which constantly insists on the idea of a superiority of the British race, and he speaks indeed of an 'aristocracy of nature'. A second important element, according to Arendt, is that racism is primarily the invention of the middle class, which 'wanted scientists who could prove that the great men, not the aristocrats, were the true representatives of the nation, in whom the "genius of the race" was personified' – a point of view which was also Disraeli's, for whom 'all is race, there is no other truth'.[7]

We may, then, in Arendt's view, range France on the one side of the divide and Germany and Britain on the other, the invention of race thinking by the nobility being counterposed to its invention by spokesmen of middle classes fired by genuine national sentiment. There is perhaps more brilliance than substance in this analysis.[8] It does, however, represent an effort to associate racism, as an ideological and political phenomenon, with, on the one hand, the work of various societies on themselves and the projects and difficulties of particular social categories, and, on the other, with the rise of nationalism – whether as part of such a movement (Germany, Britain) or as a reaction against it (France).

2. Racism as modern ideology

Louis Dumont also displayed an interest in racism as an ideology and, more particularly, as a modern ideology, 'a system of ideas and values characteristic of modern societies'.[9] But his conceptual framework differed in some respects from that proposed by Hannah Arendt. It was based, initially, on the opposition – which runs through the whole of his work – between individualism and holism. In holistic societies, based on a principle of hierarchy, the individual is subordinate to the group, which confers a status upon him or her; by contrast, the functioning of individualistic societies is to be explained by starting out from the individual, defined by his/her juridical equality with every other individual, not by his/her place or by a predetermined status.

For Dumont, holism is the rule – which he studied at length in his magisterial analysis of the caste system in India – a system which is religious in essence, based on the separation between the pure and the impure. And individualism, which can be identified in Europe and the West from the eighteenth century onwards, is the exception.

If the distinction between holism and individualism provides Dumont with the key to the emergence of racism as an ideological phenomenon, this is quite simply because he observes that it is when there is transition from the one to the other that the possibility of racism opens up. The idea may be formulated in sociological terms: racism develops in the United

States, notes Dumont, when slavery is abolished and, with it, the established social distance this involved; it is this distance racism was to reconstitute. But Dumont's reasoning owes more to political anthropology: racism appears with the rise of egalitarianism and the dissolution of holistic thought; it is a poisoned fruit of the Enlightenment, a specific product of modernity and the individualism it entails.

This reasoning – which may be deduced from his book *Homo aequalis* in particular[10] – goes deeper than the too often superficial observation of a correlation between racism and the Age of Discovery, the Enlightenment, capitalist industrialization, nationalism or colonialism; it is based, in fact, on the idea of a fundamental connection between the valorization of the individual, egalitarianism, the under-valorization of society as a totality and racism. But what is the nature of this connection? Initially, Dumont developed the idea that racism arises with the breakdown of the structure of traditional society. In his more recent writings, however, he offers a more highly developed analysis than this earlier one in which racism was ultimately regarded as crisis behaviour. The problem is, in fact, no longer seen as one of transition, or of the mutation of one societal type into another, but rather as involving the necessary and impossible cohabitation of two modes of thinking: the old holistic one with life still in it, the new individualistic one not yet triumphant. In modern societies one does indeed find remnants of premodern elements or their continued presence, beginning with the family; above all, 'the very implementation of individualistic values set in train a complex dialectic which, in very diverse fields – and in some cases from as early as the end of the eighteenth century and the beginning of the nineteenth – gave rise to combinations in which they became subtly mingled with their opposites'.[11] This idea is applied very concretely by Dumont to the 'totalitarian disease' and, more particularly, to the person of Hitler.

Though, he explains, 'that National Socialism is a modern phenomenon', we also have to take account of the fact that there was, at that stage in Germany, a 'combination of individualism and holism in which either principle took precedence according to the situation at hand'. Totalitarianism and, within it, anti-semitic racism represent 'the attempt, in a society where individualism is deeply rooted and predominant, to subordinate it to the primacy of the society as a whole' – hence the violence of the movement 'rooted in this contradiction', a contradiction which abides in 'the very promoters of the movement, torn apart as they are by conflicting forces'.[12] It is not difficult to see how, in this struggle between holism and individualism, the Jews become the privileged object of hatred and violence: Do they not symbolize individualism and modernity? Are they not, in Hitler's eyes, 'agents of destruction, individualists who were the carriers of everything he hated in modernity – anonymous and usurious money, democratic equalitarianism, and the Marxist and Bolshevik revolution'?[13] There is a smooth transition in Dumont's writings between the person of Hitler, as expressed in *Mein Kampf*, and German society. Both experience the same inner rift – both psychological and social – the same conflict of orientations between holism and individualism, the same tense longing to restore primacy to society as totality when individualism seems to be gaining the upper hand; both externalize that longing by projecting on to the Jews the individualism which is tearing them apart, an idea which ties in again with the psychoanalytic themes raised in the preceding chapter. This mechanism in which racism enables part of the individualism which a society or an individual is reluctant to accept to be expelled on to a scapegoat may perhaps even be central in the genesis of European racism, as Dumont suggests with regard, most notably, to the Comte de Boulainvilliers.[14]

Dumont's thinking is stimulating in many respects and it is not surprising that a researcher like Todorov, having examined a broad corpus of French authors over a period of two hundred and fifty years, should draw on it in the conclusion to his work.[15] In that thinking, racism is not just an 'illness' of modernity, but also an illness of the transition to modernity, one of the modalities of holism when it still possesses sufficient strength, in spite of – and, indeed, because of – its being in crisis, to permit a more or less voluntaristic attempt to turn back the clock. Dumont himself does not go so far as to assert that, once the historical transition has been achieved, modernity is not condemned to suffer racism; he wavers, sometimes rather contradictorily, between the idea that racism can be ascribed to the mutation into modernity and the notion that it is attributable to modernity itself. And, in the end, he 'confesses' his preference for hierarchical societies and joins the anti-modern camp – hence the criticism his book has received from, among others, Alain Renaut.[16] One may reject his anti-modern pessimism and contest, as Delacampagne has done, the idea that the birth of racism as an ideology is due entirely to the emergence of modernity or to the crisis of holism.[17] But his analyses, debatable as they may seem, have the immense merit of apprehending racism in its political aspects and outlining a theory of racist violence which breaks with the classical, instrumentalist approaches by suggesting that violence may be the product of a tension or a contradiction for which it provides a mode of resolution – which brings us near to analysis in terms of myth which we shall discuss below.

To study racism as an ideology in the sense of Hannah Arendt or Louis Dumont is, then, above all to inquire into its political import. But is this not to move away from other levels of analysis and perhaps even to take the view that those levels come under other categories, as though there were, in the end, no unity to the phenomenon? The notion of ideology is a powerful tool, admittedly, but is it not also restrictive, reducing the phenomenon to its political and doctrinal expression alone, and does it not leave out of account many of the manifestations of racism?

One way of replying to such objections might be to broaden the notion of ideology. This would then refer to a generalized principle of the imaginary perception of difference, a somato-biological representation of the Other, which runs not only across the whole political stage, or possibly through the whole state, but also through a variety of social relations, daily life, language and the press – including apparently the most commonplace material it covers, which informs not only doctrines and opinions but also concrete acts of discrimination, segregation or violence.

Thus, for example, in a major work, Colette Guillaumin postulates the deep unity of racist ideology, which she describes as a 'perceptual organization of the apprehension of sameness and difference', 'the crystallized state of an imaginary', and 'a latent ideological organization'.[18] Racism, which since the nineteenth century has become a central value of Western culture, then appears as a mode of biologization of social thought, which renders difference absolute by naturalizing it. One may study the historical genesis of this process, and Colette Guillaumin applies herself to that task; above all, one has to show how it functions in the present, which she also does, in particular by analysing the content of a major newspaper. Without breaking with a political approach to ideology, this broadens the mode of analysis to the social and sociological critique of the phenomenon and brings out the social relations it conceals, denies, evades or, at any event, allows to remain unnamed.

3. Racism as myth

However, is the notion of ideology, in the broad sense – transcending the political level – really the best way of designating racism, as an imaginary social construct, in sociological terms? Is not the closely related but different notion of myth more appropriate? The intellectual itinerary of Léon Poliakov suggests that we should examine this question seriously.

This historian, known primarily for his monumental *History of Anti-Semitism*,[19] has pointed up many of the neglected aspects of this very important form of racism – not the least of these being how it represents the dark side of the philosophy of the Enlightenment – and has proposed a veritable counter-history of the West, having, in Georges Élias Sarfati's words, unveiled its 'accursed share' [*part maudite*].[20] The *History of Anti-Semitism* has been criticized at times for placing excessive emphasis on 'the coherence, unity and continuity of the expressions of hostility to the Jews' and some have suggested a link between this unified vision and the highly descriptive character of the work.[21] Yet, after bringing out all the historical density of European anti-semitism, Poliakov sought to turn the perspective around: 'Whereas, in the *History of Anti-Semitism*, my aim was to examine the way Europe viewed the Jews, this time, the intention was to examine how Europe looked on itself',[22] an objective which led him to study what he calls the 'founding myths of racism'.

The main idea here is that racism is based on elaborations of myth which consist in integrating various of the elements which make up a national culture into a single image and organizing a representation of its origin.

Anti-semitic racism enables the unified and unique character of the nation to be registered. It provides the myth of origin which becomes an influential factor, a source of action, not unlike the idea of the general strike which, in the writings of Georges Sorel, is meant to provide the labour movement with the mobilizing myth it needs to achieve the highest level of its aspirations.

Before even attempting to establish the influence of myths of origin – and we have an excellent example of this type of undertaking in Anthony D. Smith's book on the ethnic origins of nations[23] – Poliakov set about a reconstruction of how they were formed, beginning with the Aryan myth, which, in Western Europe, sets an Aryan origin against a Semitic one. Poliakov's pioneering work shows that this construction, which is developed all through the nineteenth century, goes back to Antiquity.[24] He also shows that a myth has a history of its own, that it is not stabilized once and for all, but rather evolves with the historical tensions it stokes up: 'all national representations are symbolically conflict-laden', explains Poliakov, pointing out that myths of origin are 'perfectly sectarian' and that they have a great capacity for reactivation. The same myths can appear in places other than where they were formed: 'it is not in Europe, but in the countries of the Third World – or close to it – that these myths continue to make themselves felt in various guises.'[25] Not all myths produce racism, at least in its anti-semitic form. If they are to give rise to racism, it is perhaps necessary that they take a specific form in which mythic thinking provides an explanation in terms of elementary and exhaustive causality – Poliakov's 'diabolic causality', which he sees, ultimately, as lying at the root of persecution.[26] Within this perspective, anti-semitism becomes indissociable from a 'policing vision' of history, as Manès Sperber has it; it comes under the heading of demonological myths, which attribute demoniacal, conspiratorial plots or practices of witchcraft to a particular human group, without ever being troubled by the absence – even the total absence – of proof. On the contrary indeed, the conspiracy argument feeds on 'the regrettable habit of finding its most conclusive evidence in the lack of evidence, since the effectiveness of a secret society is measured by the secrecy with which it surrounds its activities. Is not the Devil's major triumph making others believe that he does not exist?'[27]

Poliakov is part, then, of a movement which he refers to as 'new historiography', which is concerned with the mythology of plots, secret societies and forces of evil which a society invents when it gives itself over to accusations of witchcraft or child-murder, or when it accuses the Jews of aspiring to control the world. The quasi-anthropological explanation based on the theme of myth provides the foundation for the historian's work, which then consists in reconstructing the invention of myths, as is done for example by Norman Cohn in his *Warrant for Genocide*,[28] or by Jacob Katz in his works on the representations of Jews and freemasons since the eighteenth century,[29] or, again, in a sense, by Pierre Birnbaum with regard to a political myth which, since the nineteenth century in France, has suggested that the Jews have been the chief beneficiaries of the Republican pact and that they have taken over the state and undermined 'true' France.[30]

It is not difficult to see that this mythological perspective we have just discussed is far more appropriate to anti-semitism than to any other form of racism. Yet it does provide a style of approach which can be broadened if one moves away somewhat from the conspiracy theme or treats that theme in terms of the more general one of *evil*, imputed to the Other in this or some other form. If the notion of myth is distinct from that of ideology in the broad sense, this is not because it offers a fundamentally different principle of analysis. Both, in fact, suggest that racism is an imaginary construct which allows the racialized group to be categorized biologically and essentialized, that is, to be treated in such a way as to detach it from all humanity and, *a fortiori*, from any social relations, either by naturalizing or diabolizing it, or doing both at the same time. The distinction between the two notions, where racism is concerned, lies rather in the processes at work in the production of an imaginary and racializing perception of the Other. The notion of ideology puts the accent on the meaning of the racist act and discourse, on the function of justification and rationalizion of the massacre, exploitation and negation of the Other which racism performs; the notion of myth stresses, rather, a particular mechanism which consists in reconciling more or less disparate and contradictory elements in an imaginary register and unifying them in a single representation. But the great strength of the two notions is the same: both account for racism's capacity to interpret everything in its own categories, whatever the reality of the facts or the rigorousness of the demonstration put up against those categories.

CONCLUSION

In order to conceptualize racism, we have to set aside the notion of race, at least as a category of analysis. This can only be done radically. Intermediate solutions, which introduce or maintain even a partial biological explanation within the field of social relations, can only produce confusion or misunderstanding. How, indeed, can we denounce the non-scientific character of the notion of race and still be a part of that important movement within sociology which, even today, is engaged in the study of 'race relations'? The conceptual slide among many writers of that school which leads them now to speak, rather, of 'ethnicity' in order, as Pierre L. Van den Berghe puts it, to 'exorcize the evil of racism' is often mere sleight of hand, so much does the catch-all notion of ethnic group allow the word 'race' to remain unspoken while scope is still to some degree accorded to physical factors, which are seen as combining with cultural features to characterize so-called 'ethnic' groups.[1] This is a point to which we shall return.

The shift by which we move from race to racism as our object naturally does not exclude the study of relations between groups defined by race; but it does demand that we affirm, without any ambiguity, the subjective, socially and historically constructed character of the recourse to that notion, which belongs to the discourse and consciousness of the social actors, and not, in any sense, to sociological analysis.

It seems to us that the social sciences have, overall (though this statement does require some degree of qualification), moved to a position from which racism may be properly constituted as an object of analysis. For the most part, they now leave out of account explanations deriving from the idea of race, even though some scope is still left for these, particularly in sociobiology, and they are sometimes reintroduced surreptitiously.

Do we, however, at this stage in our deliberations, possess a sociological theory of racism? We have so far encountered a variety of approaches and the least we can say is that there have been fundamental differences between them. Some require that we study concrete relations between groups reciprocally defined by race; others that we grasp the formation of prejudice solely as a process going on inside the individual generating the racism; yet others are concerned with the mythic structure of racism or see it as a political ideology. Perhaps we should regard each of these lines of reasoning as a partial theory awaiting integration into a broader, more general one. Yves Chevalier was tempted by such an approach and suggests, writing of anti-semitism, that the most diverse contributions be unified, insofar as they are not invalidated by the facts, within a model of interaction and systemic regulation – the scapegoating model.[2] At this stage of our deliberations, however, the idea of bringing together the various points of view we have touched upon seems very artificial, given that the paradigms on which they are based are so far apart, if not indeed irreconcilable, and that their fields of application are so clearly different, as can be seen from the radical distinction which exists between anti-semitism and the other forms of racism, a distinction also reflected in the titles of certain anti-racist organizations. How are we to postulate the theoretical unity of racism when, for example, some see prejudice as being based on a relation of domination which it formulates or rationalizes and others see it as an imaginary construct reproduced by upbringing and the family milieu? How are we to affirm the identity of phenomena which are explained, in some quarters, by a concrete relation and, in others, solely by the work of the racist actor upon him- or herself? Should we see racist doctrine, myth or ideology as providing a basis for practice, or, on the contrary, as an expression of that practice?

We shall not discover the deep unity of racism, if indeed it is possible to do so, by attempting to reconcile the available theorizations. This is why we are about to explore another approach here, starting out not from the modes of reasoning we have been able to identify in various authors, but from concrete expressions of the phenomenon, its empirical manifestations.

PART TWO

THE ELEMENTARY FORMS
OF RACISM

INTRODUCTION

If it does not seem possible, for the moment, to subsume racism under a general theory, is this not quite simply because the term brings under a single heading what is, in fact, a heterogeneous set of problems? In order to verify or refute this hypothesis, we have to go as far as possible with the analytical deconstruction of what is brought together in the notion of racism.

If such an effort is to bear fruit, two conditions have to be met. The first concerns the existence of instruments enabling us to break down what common-sense discourse – or even an insufficiently developed scientific approach – considers as a single whole. The tools which might provide possible differentiations within that whole must be reliable and robust: Chapter 5 of this book will be devoted to presenting these and satisfying us that they are capable of breaking down the overly superficial images of the phenomenon we are dealing with here.

The second condition relates not to the instruments of analysis, but the raw material to which they are applied. This must be concrete, empirically observable, tangible and sufficiently diverse that no historical instance of any importance slips through the net. Given this condition, we were tempted to proceed by examining typical situations, as in the work of John Rex (frontier situations, slavery, caste system, etc.).[1] Or to accord prime importance to processes, as in the work of Richard A. Schermerhorn, who is concerned fundamentally with the various possible modalities of integration of ethnic groups into different societies.[2] But defining typical situations or processes calls already for conceptual elaboration at a point when we need simple categories to enable us, as directly as possible, to undertake an effort of deconstruction. This is why our attempt at an analytic breakdown takes the form of a totally empirical *découpage*, a reduction to elementary, non-constructed forms of racism which are so many current and visible manifestations of the phenomenon.

We shall thus distinguish between *prejudice* – seen not, as in Chapter 3, as an explanatory or theoretical category, but as a reality more or less explicitly expressed in everyday speech or in the media and which is identifiable, if not indeed quantifiable, with the aid of sampling or questionnaire techniques[3] – *segregation*, which we shall differentiate as markedly as possible from the apparently adjacent category of *discrimination*, and, lastly, *violence*. The specialist literature offers other ways of empirically dividing up the material, ways which differ from ours in minor aspects only, not in their guiding principle. The image of racism commonly found in the literature is a three-dimensional one, including a first sub-set made up of prejudices, opinions and attitudes, a second grouping together behaviours and practices (of discrimination, segregation and violence) and a third running from arguments of a scholarly or doctrinal nature to racism as a full-blown ideology. We shall not, ourselves, return to this final sub-set, which has already been touched on in the first part of this work.[4] None of these ways of dividing up the material – including our own – is able to furnish us with a theory of racism. But each offers a convenient starting point, a concrete description on the basis of which we can attempt to establish connections between ideas and facts, between analytic categories and the realities they are supposed to elucidate.

5

LEVELS AND LOGICS OF RACISM

In certain historical experiences, racism is a weak, limited or secondary presence and it may even be more accurate, in some cases, to speak of xenophobia or inter-cultural tensions than of racism properly so-called. In others, by contrast, it sweeps all before it, structures political and social life and incites to change, conquest and war. This is why it is not without some value to attempt an overall classification at the outset. There are no conceptual pretensions to this, but it will enable us to recognize different levels of the phenomenon, varying modes of intensity, presence and integration of its elementary forms and thus identify the main axes around which to build an analytical representation of the phenomenon.

1. The empirical space of racism

It is possible, at a first approximation, to distinguish between four levels of racism.

(a) At a first level, it would be better to speak of *infra-racism* than of fully constituted racism. Here, the phenomenon is both minor and apparently disjointed. One finds the presence of doctrines, the spread of prejudices and opinions, which are often more xenophobic than strictly racist or are linked to communal rather than genuinely racial identities. There may be outbreaks of violence, but these will be diffuse and highly localized. There may also be the beginnings of segregation, though this again will be as much a social as a racial phenomenon, based, for example, in pockets where poverty and unemployment vie in importance with the marginalization of ethnic groups. Discrimination will also be encountered at times in some institutions, but it will be of a minor or shamefaced kind, or will quickly be condemned. Communication between one form of infra-racism and another will not be openly established; each will appear to conform to an autonomous logic; the links will not be clear, for example, between the activity of relatively marginal ideologues and the emergence of isolated acts of violence carried out by individuals or small groups arising out of more or less chance circumstances and guided by no very developed ideas.

(b) At a second level, racism still remains *fragmented*, but it is already distinctly more precise or assertive. It presents itself as racism, openly expressed, and can even be measured – for example, by opinion polls. The doctrine is more widespread and inspires a greater range of publications, pressure groups and theoretical groupings. Violence is more frequent and so repetitive as no longer to be regarded as a secondary phenomenon – as the action of unbalanced individuals, the product of an extremely fortuitous situation or a very specific conjuncture. Segregation or discrimination are also more marked, being perceptible in various fields of social life or registered visibly in space. The whole phenomenon forms a single entity, but still seems disjointed, as if society were experiencing a single impulse, without finding the binding agent to provide a concrete unity for its various expressions.

(c) That binding agent appears at a third level when racism becomes the principle of action of a political or para-political force; when racism itself becomes *political*, inspiring debates and pressures, mobilizing broad sectors of the population, creating a context favourable to an increase in instances of violence or using that violence as an instrument in a strategy for seizing power. At this stage, the political movement serves as an accumulator of opinions and prejudices, but also orients and develops them; it proclaims its adherence to doctrinal elements which are now no longer marginalized, acquires organic intellectuals, claims a place within an ideological tradition or founds one, whilst at the same time calling for concrete discriminatory measures or a project of racial segregation.

(d) Lastly, a final level is achieved when the state itself comes to be organized on racist lines, develops policies and programmes of mass exclusion, destruction or discrimination, calls on scholars or intellectuals to contribute to this effort, mobilizes the resources of the law to enforce its racial categories and structures its institutions in terms of these categories. Racism becomes *total* if those who direct the state succeed in subordinating everything to it: science, technology, institutions, but also the economy, moral and religious values, the historical past and military expansion; if it shapes all fields of political and social life, at all levels, without any possibility of debate or protest. It is total, to employ a different terminology, to the extent that it *fuses* all kinds of diversities into a single dynamic and jettisons everything that accords the racialized group a place – even a very inferior one – in society. As a sociological pattern, total racism is only ever achieved by being embodied in a state. But it may be encountered in groups functioning on that model, reproducing the principle of the state on a smaller scale and doing so, consequently, in a mode that is both terroristic and sectarian.

When represented in this way, the empirical space of racism does not, of itself, enable us to confirm or disconfirm the hypothesis of the fundamental unity of the phenomenon. We can certainly see that, in the case of fragmented racism and infra-racism, there is some distance between the elementary forms of which these are composed, but we cannot deduce from this that there is, at bottom, an irreducible difference between these forms; we certainly perceive different degrees of importance or intensity each time we move from one level to another, but we are still unable to say whether or not they allow us to conceive racism as a single, continuous phenomenon.

2. Fragmentation and fusion

It is now possible, however, to introduce a first principle of analytical differentiation, based on a fundamental criterion: whether or not the racism in question is of a directly political character. Everything changes the moment racism becomes, strictly speaking, a political phenomenon, and changes even more, indeed, when it becomes a state phenomenon. The transition to the political level does not change the content of racism in its fundamentals, whether that racism postulates a difference between supposed human races or a hierarchy among them. But it unifies practices, discourses and effects which, without it, would scarcely have any way of being brought together. From this point of view, fragmented racism and, *a fortiori*, infra-racism are to be distinguished radically from political racism and its tendency, in extreme cases, to create fusion.

In its fragmented state, racism may be present across institutions, may give rise to violence, may be the force inspiring statements of doctrine or currents of thinking; it may be widespread, particularly in the form of prejudice. It may inspire behaviour on a massive scale – in the housing market, for example – and lead to *de facto* segregation. In its most forthright forms, it may imprint itself upon the social structure and constitute a central principle of stratification, thus making it indissociable from relations of domination. But, so long as it does not rise to the strictly political level, so long as it bumps up against that political level but finds no outlets there, so long as it does not find the agents for its active institutionalization – intellectuals, religious leaders and, most importantly, political movements – there is no possibility of it becoming a mobilizing force.

By contrast, political racism provides projects and programmes. It synthesizes the diffuse elements which make up fragmented racism, but, above all, it structures them ideologically, gives them new-found meaning and a broader scope. It facilitates their transformation, radicalization and advance. It legitimates acts and practices which may have existed beforehand, but are now afforded helpful conditions and a favourable climate. Even if it does not call explicitly or directly for violence, it provides a context which permits or fuels it. Such violence is no longer incongruous; it expresses feelings which the protagonist knows he or she is not alone in experiencing; it is not dissociated from more general positions which have become, to some degree, representative. Political racism abolishes more or less entirely the distance which, in fragmented racism, separates thoughts from acts, consciousness from action, ideas from their realization. And, by abolishing that distance, it creates the conditions for a new dynamic. The fusion of total racism represents the privileged moment when the phenomenon seems to have become an irresistible force, a boundless, limitless logic of action.

Yet we must point out that this moment is itself likely to be transcended, not only because the actor runs up against external obstacles but also because, having once become a logic of action, racism destroys the elements on which it was built and developed. Thus, for example, in Nazism, the conjoining of the scientific and the political – as Michael Pollak has shown in his subtle analysis – initially produced an interaction to which the 'atrocities committed in the name of improving the race'[1] may be imputed, an interaction all the more decisive in that it allowed no scope for debate either in the scientific or the political field. But the scientists, who at first derived enormous advantages from their proximity to power – if only in terms of resources, and research and career opportunities – also had to sanction or validate non-scientific practices, were subject to surveillance and monitoring and saw the most mediocre among them, if not indeed the outright charlatans, acquire prestige and influence to the detriment of the most able. Benno Müller-Hill provides a good description of this process, which led to the perversion and then negation of science, for example among psychiatrists who, despite their vocation to cure mental patients, were employed to sterilize and, most importantly, eliminate them. Their discipline lost its *raison d'être* – and not only that since, in concrete terms, 'for the psychiatrists of provincial mental hospitals losing their patients meant losing their wards and often the loss of the entire hospital; and with that went their position and their power'.[2]

Prejudices, discrimination, segregation, violence or doctrine sometimes seem so disconnected that, on a first analysis, one can only register the distance between them and, at best, present that distance as a paradox. This paradox is often exemplified in the psycho-sociology textbooks by a study carried out many years ago by Richard T. LaPiere. In an article of 1934, he tells how, having travelled in the company of a Chinese couple through many states of the USA, he went to 184 restaurants and stayed in 66 hotels with them, without ever meeting with rejection, except in one case – and that not at all clear-cut.[3] However, when he sent the restaurateurs and hoteliers concerned a questionnaire on their usual behaviour, more than 90 per cent of the respondents indicated that they would not serve Chinese. LaPiere's study, which has been confirmed by others conducted on the same lines, cannot, however, be taken to point up a paradoxical contradiction. In fact, it perfectly illustrates our point, that only when racism reaches the political and state level does the phenomenon aquire cohesion. Otherwise it remains fragmented and, ultimately, contradictory. Gordon W. Allport saw this very clearly when, in his commentary on LaPiere's experiment, he framed the hypothesis that: 'Where clear conflict exists, with law and conscience on the one side, and with custom and prejudice on the other, discrimination is practiced chiefly in covert and indirect ways, and not primarily in face-to-face situations where embarrassment would result.'[4]

A writer as important as Colette Guillaumin forcefully asserts that racism constitutes a system. In her view, 'meaning does not exist in itself, but in the concrete act';[5] one cannot 'separate the doctrine from the material facts';[6] 'theory and behaviour are rooted in a shared system of signs, even if it is mediated in different registers'.[7] But, in fragmented racism, the system Guillaumin speaks of becomes dislocated and the expression of meaning is restrained by the absence of favourable political conditions; concrete acts are masked or their meaning is distorted, and the relative disjunction between theory and behaviour, even if both are prompted by the same deep meanings, prohibits the emergence of processes which only acquire force and specificity when meaning and act, doctrine and material facts, theory and behaviour are politically unified and reconciled.

It is often said that there is in everyday speech a continuous thread running from the least significant anti-semitic remark to Auschwitz and the gas chambers. This postulate fails to grasp the radical nature of the leap involved in the transition to the political level and the fundamental role played by the agents of that transition. The most worrying thing for a society is not the existence of a fragmented – albeit potently established – racism, but the existence of political actors capable of carrying racism across the line where it becomes a force for collective mobilization, a force which may possibly be capable of going on to capture state power. Such actors may be openly and fundamentally racist from the outset, but this is not a necessary condition. It is enough for their action to have within it the seeds of a racist project – even a very limited or incidental one at the outset – for that seed, in time, to bear its poisoned fruit. This is why political populism in particular – which combines all sorts of meanings in an unstable equilibrium, with, as a rule, a narrow initial space for a racist thematics – represents such a great danger. The evolution of such a movement may in fact very well end in a greater predominance of racism, to the detriment of other meanings which have turned out in practice not to be effective or, at least, not sufficiently effective.

3. Difference and inequality

At the beginning of the 1980s, both by its content and its very title, a work by Martin Barker gave rise, in Britain, to the notion of a 'new racism'.[8] The discourse of this 'new racism', according to Barker, is one element in the ideological revision undertaken by the Conservative Party in the 1970s. That discourse enabled it to focus on immigration, perceived as an agent of the destruction of the British nation, and to theorize the idea that every national or ethnic community is a specific expression of human nature which is neither superior nor inferior, but different.[9]

Similarly, Pierre-André Taguieff in France has shown how, since the 1970s, a 'differentialist' racism has been constituted within the doctrinal field by the writings of the GRECE and the Club de l'Horloge* and in the

---

* *Translator's note*: Right-wing intellectual groupings of the Far Right which have been influential since the late 1970s in propagating theories based on socio-biology.

political field by identity-based discourse and the appeal to a right to a difference of identity, as formulated by the Front national in a national-populist mode not far removed from that of the Conservative Party as described by Barker.[10]

This reactivation of a theme which is not all that new, since one finds it in the most radical positions of the proponents of cultural relativism since the turn of the century, stresses the link between culture and community and racism. It has the great virtue, as Taguieff has quite brilliantly shown, of introducing a new analytical distinction – not, in this case, by contrasting two levels of racism (the political and the infra-political), but by pointing up the existence of two 'logics of racialization', two possible 'series': 'auto-racialization–difference–purification/cleansing–extermination', on the one hand, and 'hetero-racialization–inequality–domination–exploitation', on the other.[11]

This distinction, in which we shall leave aside the questionable opposition between auto– and hetero-racialization, is a basic one: it strikes, at the deepest level, against the hypothesis of the unity of racism. It may be transcribed into two registers: into the terms of the history and analysis of ideas and ideologies and into those of sociology.

In the first register, it presents us with a two-fold phenomenon, formed by two axes which are in every way opposed to one another. This is the classical pairing, not solely confined to racism, of the universalist approach, a strong version of which is provided by evolutionist thinking, and the relativist approach, as expressed for example in a certain kind of cultural anthropology or, alternatively, in the historicism which dominated nineteenth-century German philosophy. Within this perspective, there is not one racism, but two. The first of these believes that there is only one universal, that of the dominant race, to which other races can only be subordinated in relations of domination. The second postulates that there are as many universals as there are cultures and, behind each culture, races. It is not possible to rank or compare universals and each of these represents so many potential threats to the others. Racism, in this case, no longer means relations of domination, but rather the setting apart, the exclusion and, in the extreme case, the destruction of races which are thought to pose a threat. This highlighting of two logics of racism represents a decisive step forward for understanding a number of historical paradoxes. Thus, for example, a number of nineteenth-century race theorists – Gobineau, Le Bon, Broca – were hostile to colonization, which set in place an inegalitarian racism but also ran the risk of promoting interbreeding and thus running counter to differentialist positions.

In the second register, the distinction between a difference-based and an inequality-based racism relates to what are also much more general patterns familiar to sociologists, to two general orders of problem which they long since learned not to confuse. The idea of inequality is, in fact, merely one formulation among others of the division of a society and the relations of domination within it; the idea of difference, on the other hand, relates to the unity of a social body or of one of its sub-sets, whether this latter be defined in the broad terms of culture, community and identity or in the more precise terms of nation, religion and, ultimately, race. To recognize that two logics of racism exist is, therefore, to recognize the existence of two logics of action, the one governed more by a society's work on itself – its social conflicts and the phenomena of stratification and upward and downward mobility within it – the other closer to community movements, to calls for homogeneity, purity, the expulsion of the hetero-geneous and the different. It is, to draw on the vocabulary of the sociology of action developed by Alain Touraine, to forge theoretical links – which should, none the less, not be over-simplified – between inegalitarian racism and social action, on the one hand, and differentialist racism and historical action, on the other.[12]

The fact that we must assert the conceptual independence of these two axes does not mean that they necessarily function separately in historical practice. This is, indeed, far from being the case. A great many experi-ences combine the logic of difference with that of inequality, either by juxtaposing them or by seeking to integrate them into a single political formula, as was the case with apartheid up to the end of the 1980s. One also finds cases where one of the two logics gives way to the other. For example, an inequality-based racism, based on relations of economic exploitation, may be supplanted by an identity-based racism when these relations break down.

This brings us to a final series of remarks. If, most of the time, racism combines inferiorization and differentiation, this is because the mechan-isms of its production necessarily entail both of these to a greater or lesser extent. If it is pushed to the extreme, a logic of inferiorization also entails processes of rejection and setting apart, and, by the same token, a logic of differentiation only takes on a racist coloration if its target is not totally external to the culture or community concerned, that is, if it can be included in social relations, however mythical these may be. Let us put this another way: in order to be effective, a pure logic of inferiorization needs to be backed up by a logic of differentiation; and a pure logic of differentiation, if it does not end in some kind of inferiorizing of its victim, issues either in something other than racism – in war, for example – or in the physical destruction of the racialized group, which is, historically, an exceptional outcome. This is probably why, in the lecture to which we have already referred, Claude Lévi-Strauss can speak in defence of cultural distance: there is, in effect, scarcely any racism between cultures which do not communicate, between groups which do not overlap within ensembles in which meeting necessarily ends in relations of inferiorization.

When racism is weak and fragmented, the two basic logics are often themselves dissociated, and it is not rare for only one of them to be genuinely present. When racism raises itself to the political level, however, when it tends towards fusion, this fusion signifies also that, however contradictory they may seem, the two logics are jointly present.

We must therefore isolate analytically the two basic logics of racism, but we must also be aware that there is no historical experience of any great magnitude in which they are not found in combination. However this may be, we now have two analytical tools at our disposal: the one distinguishing between levels – the political and the infra-political – the other, the import of which will be explained in more detail in Part Three of this book, specifying two logics of action. We are now going to put these tools to work to examine the elementary forms of racism.

6
PREJUDICE

In Chapter 3, we stressed the importance of the new angle generated by moving from a sociology of 'race relations' to approaches centred more on the racist actor and the prejudices and personality of that actor.

But does this mean that we possess a satisfactory theory of racial prejudice? Most researchers, working within a rationalist tradition, regard prejudice as error, as a judgement which constructs the Other in a predetermined way without being informed by concrete experience or affected by what that experience contributes or by criticism, however rational it may be. But the sources of prejudice vary considerably from one writer to another.[1] Some, as we have seen, emphasize the personality of the prejudiced individual and are interested in the authoritarian syndrome described by Theodor Adorno, the structural weakness discussed by Erich Fromm and the dogmatism, irrespective of the content of the dogma, analysed by Milton Rokeach.[2] This point of view tends to decontextualize racism from the social conditions in which it is expressed, and studies such as Thomas Pettigrew's in the 1950s clearly show that its limitations soon become apparent. Comparing the differences in attitude towards blacks and Jews observed in South Africa, and in the southern and northern states of the USA, Pettigrew demonstrates, in effect, that these are not easily explained in terms of authoritarian personality since, for example, non-Jewish whites in the south and north of the USA are very similar where anti-semitism and authoritarianism (measured on Adorno's famous 'F scale') are concerned, but differ considerably when it comes to their anti-black prejudice.[3]

By contrast, other writers, moving away from the theme of personality, stress the social and cultural determinants of prejudice. Thus, for example, Richard A. Schermerhorn asserts that prejudice 'is a product of *situations*, historical situations, economic situations, political situations; it is not a little demon that emerges in people simply because they are depraved'.[4] This formulation is, however, still vague and brings us up against an enormous range of propositions relating to the factors producing prejudice: every society, through its conflicts, structural relations of domination, forms of stratification and social mobility, and every culture, with its values, history, traditions and tendencies to ethnocentrism,[5] generates prejudices which leave their mark, even on the most critical minds.[6] Most of the time, prejudice is viewed as a product of error or mystification, but this view is rejected by some, who regard it not as a false or alienated perception of reality but, for example, as a value or cultural characteristic. Thus, as Gérard Lemaine and James S. Jackson have noted, from the 1940s onwards, a writer as important as Warner stressed the idea that 'racism is one value of White society, no more irrational than another, and what is crucial is the desire for endogamy, the rules of descent and the social categorization of race'.[7] At other times, theory stresses the functional character of the racial prejudice: does it not, for example, serve to legitimate and rationalize social domination?

Examining the various classical approaches to prejudice, one quickly arrives at the view that they form a heterogeneous collection. Gordon W. Allport produced a tabular representation of these, distinguishing between six different theories (the historical, socio-cultural and situational approaches, the approach via personality dynamics and structure, the phenomenological approach and the approach via stimulus object).[8] And even if Otto Klineberg suggests that there is some interdependence between these theories, which might actually be seen as corresponding to different levels of analysis,[9] one cannot but be left somewhat perplexed, as for example when reading Allport: either racial prejudice is a multi-dimensional reality which falls within the ambit of several theories or levels without any overarching unity, since each theory or level calls on its own autonomous conceptual system, or it is, in fact, an elementary form of racism, but there is neither any intellectual consensus on – nor compelling definition of – its nature.

Yet this elementary form does possess an empirical reality. The expression of racial prejudice is commonly observed in conversation and in the press; we know how to hunt down prejudices in discourse analysis, how to quantify them in surveys. They have also been analysed in an important variant form – rumour. We might assume that this latter is a product of comparable cognitive mechanisms, but with the particular feature of adding to the preconception of the Other the elaboration and dissemination not merely of characteristics, but also of facts and proposing a narrative which is presented as concrete, undeniable and authentic and confirms or reinforces the prejudice. Isolating the essence of the phenomenon would not seem to get us very far here, and the idea of identifying all the social, cultural or psychological factors which create prejudice can only lead to a kind of inventory without any great coherence; on the other hand, it is possible, on a first approach, to situate prejudice within social relations and to see it as a subjective dimension of action.

1. Domination and prejudice

An important intellectual tradition, informed largely by the various forms of exploitation and domination of blacks in American society, contributes the first elements of an understanding of the phenomenon. Within this tradition, prejudice is the direct expression of structural social relations, whether described in terms of class or, rather, of stratification. It provides the members of the dominant group with the means to rationalize their position, which it grounds and perpetuates ideologically; it makes it easy for them, as John Dollard indicated in his study of 'Southerntown', to gain advantages in economic terms or in terms of prestige or sexuality. It makes extreme forms of exploitation or violence psychologically tolerable to those who benefit from them. But is it at the origin of these things or is it not, rather, a consequence of them? This is a question which keeps coming up again and again, for example in the debate on slavery in the USA.[10] This perspective none the less makes a connection between prejudices and the interests of social groups, and suggests, when the interminable discussions of the order of causation are put aside, a link which may take two main forms: prejudice may either attest to a predominantly offensive attitude – maintaining or reinforcing domination – or relate to a defensive one, to a fear, for example, of seeing the social and racial structure transformed to the advantage of the dominated – and racialized – group.

The idea of a certain functionality of prejudice, rooted in the social structure, possible changes to which it accompanies (or precedes) – changes relating to very real groups (whites and blacks in the American case) – is most often nuanced and does not exclude an attempt to create theoretical links with approaches in terms of personality and individual psychology. It may also take a rather abrupt turn, producing a perspective much more instrumentalist than functional. Prejudice then becomes a tool employed strategically by actors who use it to maximize their benefits and minimize their costs. This idea is developed in an original way by Teun A. Van Dijk to study the way racism is communicated.[11] Analysing the content of 180 interviews carried out in California and the Netherlands, Van Dijk observes that prejudice is of service in what may be limited interactions – those of daily life, in particular – but that these interviews express a structural property of the societies under consideration, which enables individuals belonging to the dominant group to deploy strategies of persuasion and self-presentation. By expressing oneself in a negative way about others, one presents oneself in a positive light, has a line of argument at one's disposal and establishes communication with one's own.

In this perspective, which is both interactionist and instrumentalist, prejudice is one element in processes of communication that are also learning processes operating through interpersonal relations within the majority group, as well as under the influence of the mass media.

But can we take this idea of an instrumentality of prejudice very far? In fact, the more the idea is asserted, the more prejudice seems to come under the heading of calculation and rational choice. The notion of prejudice may ultimately lose all content if racism is to be explained in terms of the advantage the racist derives from it; this is why the radical proposals of Michael Hechter in his defence of rational choice theory applied to the study of race relations, or the more nuanced and cautious arguments of Michael Banton in a number of his writings which also make reference to this line of thinking, seem to us to cast very little light on racism so far as the aspect of imaginary construction or representation in the psycho-sociological sense is concerned.[12] Moreover, to stay within this perspective for a moment, is there not also a substantial price to pay for racial prejudice? Is not 'prejudice', as Simpson and Yinger assert in their classic work, 'an expensive luxury in terms of the *prejudiced person's own total interests and values*'?[13]

From the point where the social structure is also a racial structure, in which oppositions experienced in terms of race cut across forms of domination, conflict or social stratification by whatever principle these latter are organized, then, even if it is excessive to adopt an instrumental point of view, it is not at all absurd to assume a direct connection between the expression of prejudice and the fact of belonging to a dominant group.

However, such an assumption clearly does not fit every situation and is perhaps less solidly based than one might think.

2. Loss and reconstitution of meaning

'Poor white' racism – as we have seen in Tocqueville, Weber or Myrdal – enables a socially threatened actor, who is falling down the social scale or at the bottom of it, to create a distance from – and sense of superiority to – a group from which that actor is otherwise barely separated in strictly social terms. This mechanism applies to a concrete situation in which whites and blacks are jointly present, but it does not necessarily call into existence, at the outset, a racial or social relationship between the two groups: it may contribute to creating such a relationship if it does not exist. But this already moves us away, to some degree, from the idea that prejudice is unfailingly the mark of a relation that is already constructed, a domination anchored in facts.

Another example will help us to clarify an argument which, though it does not cause us to question the line of reasoning just outlined above, provides a different perspective. It is provided, most ably, by the analysis of the so-called 'rumour in Orléans' which Edgar Morin presents in the work of that name.[14]

In the late 1960s a rumour spread through the city of Orléans to the effect that the Jewish shopkeepers were drugging young female customers and despatching them into the white slave trade. This anti-semitic rumour treats social and cultural themes in a manner characteristic of mythology and Morin shows that it attests to a fear of the change and modernity which the new culture of the sixties or the May '68 movement represented for what was, in relative terms, a provincial backwater. Drugs and white slavery, for example, can be read as a way of dealing with an undeclared conflict between the desire on the part of young girls to travel and be part of modern culture and a traditional provincialism which could not but be opposed to that desire. It is clearly not by chance that prejudice is directed here against Jews. The Jew, indeed, provides the classic embodiment, reactivated for the occasion, of the conflict or contradiction between tradition and modernity, or between particularism and universalism, and serves as the scapegoat which enables this type of tension to be resolved mythically. He is a 'two-faced monster', at once honorable and modern, but rapacious; he is like everyone else, but belongs to a mysterious world; he lives in the heart of the city and yet he is alien.[15]

It was found in Orléans that the rumour had nothing to do with any economic or social conflict to which it might be said to have given direct expression. It was not a pendant to any form of pressure – from non-Jewish commerce, for example – to eliminate effective competition; it was not part of any real tension between Jewish shopowners and other local actors; it did not provide the key to any relation of this type. In its own way, it was a means of dealing with the combination of a fear of modernity and a lack – 'an emptiness at the very heart of the town. Different kinds of emptiness – ethical, political, affective, existential . . .,' for which, as Morin tells us, the rumour compensated.[16] The rumour constructed a meaning where the signposts were confused or absent. Prejudice here arises out of a loss of meaning which it makes up for with an imaginary reconstruction, fuelled by a reactivation of the traditional figure of evil – the Jew.

We may view this mechanism as being to some degree a general one, and conclude that racial prejudice is, in many cases, a way of managing meaning which proceeds by substituting a non-social signification for a social category when this latter is destabilized, weakened or exhausted. This mode of managing meaning consists of two elements. In a first phase, the potential for such a thing appears where social or inter-communal relations are destroyed or are difficult to constitute, as when the American 'poor whites' are seized by a sense of social decline or when the provincial way of life of Orléans is disturbed by the irruption of the new culture (the 'breach' [brèche] to which Morin refers in another book).[17] In a second phase, it is concretized by the actor's settling into a non-social – in this case, racial – identity, the substrate for which it* finds either in a heritage of culture and history or by over-valorizing its own phenotype to the detriment of another. The prejudice is not grounded here in the strength of the dominant party in a social or inter-cultural relationship, but in the combination of two elements: on the one hand, the crisis of the actor, the weakness of that actor and its sense that it is declining or threatened, and, on the other, its capacity to extract from its fund of historical or cultural reference, or from the manifest inferiority of a group which is itself already racialized, the elements of a non-social identity which is negative for the Other – classed as evil and inferior – but positive for the racist actor.

---

* *Translator's note*: Since the social actors to which Wieviorka refers are not necessarily individuals, they will be referred to subsequently – not too artificially, I hope – in impersonal terms.

3. 'Symbolic' racism

When racism clearly runs through a society and its institutions and, in particular, when it is associated with concrete forms of domination, the mechanism we have just presented is definitely less visible and less present than when the racist phenomenon is emerging, in the process of consti- tution or undergoing a marked transformation. In the United States, where those who were the pioneers of the measurement of prejudice and racial attitudes – researchers like Emory Bogardus and Eugene L. Hartley – succeeded in identifying a pattern of prejudice which is 'practically an American institution',[18] racial prejudice is written into the social structure and the process of *loss of meaning* and *reconstitution of meaning* is less decisive or necessary than that of the *reproduction* of prejudice – by way of the socialization of children, for example. This does not, however, mean that the prejudice is not subject to changes in content, as is attested by the lively nature of the work which has been going on since the 1970s on what is said to be the most recent form of the racist phenomenon in that country – so-called 'symbolic racism'.

The 'symbolic racism' school of thinking developed out of the realization that during the 1950s and 1960s civil rights struggles, campaigns against school segregation, the rise of black movements, the strengthening of the position of the black middle classes – if not indeed of the black bourgeoisie – or urban policies modified not only the political life of the country and the situation of the blacks, but also the racial prejudices of the whites. Prejudice, in its classical forms, is in decline. In 1942, for example, only 42 per cent of whites believed blacks had the same level of intelligence as whites, as opposed to 78 per cent in 1956; only 42 per cent of whites felt that blacks should have the same job opportunities as whites, but in 1972 the figure was 95 per cent. The crudest prejudices are losing their hold, but in 1978 only 25 per cent of whites believed that the federal government should ensure that white and black children attended the same schools, whereas, in 1966, the figure was 48 per cent.[19] We have thus moved from heavy-handed prejudices to more subtle forms, which constitute a 'sym- bolic racism' with very specific characteristics: rejection of crude stereo- types and the most visible discrimination; refusal of racial change for ostensibly non-racial reasons; a feeling that blacks 'are pushing too hard' and 'getting on too quickly' by virtue of a 'reverse discrimination' which disadvantages whites; denial of the idea of segregation, since blacks are said to have the same access as whites to the jobs and housing markets.[20] There is, in this new racism, the idea that the blacks are violating or perverting American values – that they are abusing the welfare state, for example, instead of playing the game of individual competition and relying on their own resources and merits – that they are bringing the government and the media to bear excessively in their own cause – themes which, we may note in passing, are not far removed from what is often heard in France with regard to immigration.

But the development which allows us to oppose a new, 'symbolic' racism, rooted more in the middle classes, to the old lower-class racism does not imply an increased dissociation between the consciousness of the bearers of prejudice and the social and political organization of American racism; it seems, rather, to accompany changes in the way racism is organized, at the same time, perhaps, as giving expression, more specifically, to phenomena of relative downward mobility which particularly affected the middle classes in the 1970s and 1980s.[21] This kind of prejudice, which falls under the heading of inegalitarian racism, is certainly resistant to rational criticism or to confrontation with the facts; but the very changes within it indicate that it maintains a certain contact with reality, and, though distorting that reality, does not become detached from it and take on a wholly mythical, imaginary character. Indeed, it attests to a certain capacity on the part of the actor to advance rational explanations or present facts which advert to very real social problems: it is not untrue to say that busing in fact imposes very long journeys on children, nor is it absurd to assert that a school with a very high level of foreigners who do not speak the national language penalizes the other children. By contrast, the prejudice of 'differentialist' racism can function without having to preserve any kind of connection with reality or adapt to its transformations. Most importantly, that racism evinces a disjunction between the social, political or cultural phenomena out of which it arises and those it constructs, in an imaginary mode, with the aid of mythic narratives – as in the case of the Orléans rumour – or by way of procedures based very broadly on the scapegoating mechanism. There, the strength of the prejudice is all the greater for the gap between its sociological sources and its ultimate expression being so wide, for there being such a massive loss of meaning at the point at which it forms, and for the social or other relations in which the actor could relocate him- or herself being so far out of reach.

To return for a moment to Edgar Morin's account, the Orléans rumour had a short life-cycle and soon fell apart: 'Fantasy transformed itself first into a myth, then into sheer delirium, after which it once more became fantasy, while the myth left behind numerous mini-myths, by way of legacy.'[22] This is characteristic of a transient phenomenon, governed by a social change which the population of Orléans became afraid to participate in, before it had the possibility of doing so. The prejudice blew up out of all proportion and then subsided, at least in its outward expression. In other situations – where the transformation takes longer, goes deeper and leaves a large number of misfits, who are incapable of finding a place in the new pattern of cultural and social relations, culturally or socially high and dry – racial prejudice is much more likely not just to become established or develop but also to become an obsession or a torment for its proponents.

Which brings us, in the end, to a genuine paradox. The more indissociably linked racism is to tangible social relations, the less it is possible for the prejudice as such to escape the consciousness of the actors. What is then called 'prejudice' is an expression of that consciousness, which accompanies concrete forms of domination and evolves as these forms themselves are transformed. By contrast, the more racism arises out of a process of the loss of meaning and its imaginary reconstitution, and the more it constructs a mythical image of an enemy – which it naturalizes, essentializes, biologizes or demonizes – the greater is the disjunction between the social and cultural problems within which it develops and the mythical relations it invents, and the more it is alien as prejudice to the consciousness of its bearer. When prejudice corresponds, even in a limited way, to concrete relations, it is less opaque to the consciousness of the actor than when it is constructed in an imaginary register, as in the – paroxysmal – case of the Jewless anti-semitism which has developed in contemporary Poland, one of whose most astounding characteristics is that, although it is very much present in the language of its protagonists, they are always surprised to be accused of it or are, at least, surprised at not being understood when they criticize the Jews.

Prejudice always expresses the consciousness of the actor, but that consciousness is never totally reducible to the prejudice, nor totally alien to it. It is predominantly the one or the other, depending on whether the racism functions, on the one hand, against the backcloth of a single set of social relations and concrete forms of domination, or, on the other, operates in two registers – a real one, where the racialized group plays little part, and a phantasmatic one, where, by contrast, it takes on the central role.

SEGREGATION, DISCRIMINATION

Segregation and discrimination are both concrete manifestations of racism, but a clear analytic distinction has to be made between them. The former involves keeping the racialized group apart, setting aside designated spaces for it which it may only leave under certain, more or less restrictive, conditions; the latter consists in imposing differential treatment on the group in various fields of social life, a treatment in which the group itself participates, along lines which render it inferior.

In practice, segregation and discrimination may be combined, as in South Africa, where the term 'apartheid' also designated a form of organization of economic production which made the blacks not only a segregated group, but also one that was socially dominated. On the other hand, they may also tend to become dissociated, in processes where one of the two logics wins out over the other. Thus, for example, the Nazi experience ended not only in absolute segregation – the Polish ghettos and the concentration camps – but also in the destruction of those gathered together in this way, to the detriment, if one dare use such terms, of an economic exploitation which, though carried out on a grand scale, increasingly turned out to be secondary to the plans for the final solution.

In less extreme situations, the two logics feed on each other so much and are so complementary, at the end of what are sometimes paradoxical processes, that it is not always easy to distinguish between the two. Thus, for example, the historian C. Van Woodward has shown how the economic and social transformations at the end of the last century in the southern states of the USA simultaneously gave rise to racial discrimination in industry and, under pressure from the lower-class whites, the segregationist measures of the Jim Crow laws.[1] Similarly, one cannot but be struck by the creeping tendency in contemporary France towards not simply discrimination against immigrants, but their segregation.[2]

Segregation and discrimination are empirical terms and do not correspond to clear analytic categories. This seems particularly true of discrimination, which is contested as a concept, if not as a reality, by an important school of thought which is neo-classical in inspiration. The leading figure in this school, Thomas Sowell, calls on us not to confuse discrimination with exploitation, and brings out the plurality of meanings attaching to a notion which, as was clearly seen by Pierre-André Taguieff, is in danger of designating only 'conceptually empty positions of principle and formal moral attitudes applying to all possible social situations and not touching precisely on any in particular'.[3] But let us not be misled here. Sowell's concern is not to stress the emptiness of the notion but, mainly, to challenge its misuse, by drawing on and developing Gary Becker's classical argument that the free-market economy, based on competition, prevents racial discrimination from occurring. According to this argument, one could expect such discrimination to be more widely present in public organizations, which do not have to concern themselves with productivity and profit.[4] This is a position which coincides, in many respects, with the prejudices described in the literature on 'symbolic racism' and is not particularly demanding so far as the facts are concerned, as Judith Shapiro has shown in her devastating critique of Sowell's *Markets and Minorities*.[5] Everyday, common-sense usage of the words 'discrimination' and 'segregation' is often confused and the anti-racist vulgate does misuse these terms, but this is no reason to ignore the very tangible realities which fall, if only partially, under the heading of these two elementary forms of racism.

1. Segregation

Segregation inscribes racism in space; it leaves its mark on the geopolitical organization of a country or the more limited organization of a town. It produces spatial patterns, either by the operation of spontaneous social mechanisms and of individual behaviours in which social and residential mobility intersect against a background of racism, or by the intervention of local or national institutions, of laws, regulations and acts of violence which are tolerated to varying degrees by the political powers that be.

But not all segregation is, in fact, necessarily racial or imposed and segregation may itself be continued in logics in which the notion of race becomes secondary and other categories, social and economic rather than biological and physical, are determinant. The American experience, as analysed since the pioneering works of the Chicago School, will help us to illustrate and refine this point.

1. Ethnic segregation

The Chicago sociologists, who were the first to study the phenomena of spatial segregation in concrete terms, did not look, in the first instance, for the expression of any kind of racism in that segregation. Their main aim, within an ecological perspective, was to offer models of the occupation of urban space, and sometimes even to propound genuine laws of town and city development. Hence Ernest W. Burgess's formulation of his famous 'zonal hypothesis', which, in his view, explains how cities grow outward from their central business districts.[6] 'In the expansion of the city,' he explains, 'a process of distribution takes place which sifts and sorts and relocates individuals and groups by residence and occupation. The resulting differentiation of the cosmopolitan American city into areas is typically all from one pattern.'[7] This differentiation, which relates principally to the large cities of the northern USA, was initially seen in ethnic terms: segregation was governed by migratory movements and the quasi-spontaneous gathering together of the newcomers by community of origin – Polish, Italian, etc. This is the most visible expression, since it is a spatial one, of the American 'non-melting pot', in which various ethnic minorities – that is, minorities defined by national or religious origins, not by race – co-habit within a space in which each can define itself in communal terms. Most importantly, this is regarded as a positive phenomenon: 'segregation', explains Burgess, 'offers the group, and thereby the individuals who compose the group, a place and a role in the total organization of city life'.[8] There is scarcely any basic distinction here between the Jews and other ethnic minorities who came over to found – and participate in – the American nation and its democracy, and in this perspective the Jewish ghetto is regarded, if not entirely favourably, then at least with ambivalence and is seen as comparable with the neighbourhoods of other minorities. In his classic work on the ghetto, Louis Wirth extends that evaluation back far beyond contemporary American experience to the formation of ghettos in medieval Europe. The ghetto, he explains, was not the product of a political decision on the part of the state or the church, but the 'unwitting crystallization of needs and practices rooted in the customs and heritages, religious and secular, of the Jews themselves. Long before it was made compulsory, the Jews lived in separate parts of the cities in the Western lands, of their own accord.'[9]

Here, where it is ethnically based, spatial segregation is a quasi-natural process, though it is also desired by the very people who are building or rebuilding communities. It affords them the warmth and protection of a living and, in some cases, diversified culture; it offers them economic and political resources. And, though it is sometimes experienced as oppressive, as closed in on itself and set apart from modernity, it is none the less far from being totally shut off. Segregation itself, explains Robert Park,

> tends to facilitate the mobility of the individual man. The processes of segregation establish moral distances which make the city a mosaic of little worlds which touch but do not interpenetrate. This makes it possible for individuals to pass quickly and easily from one moral milieu to another, and encourages the fascinating but dangerous experiment of living at the same time in several different contiguous, but otherwise widely separated, worlds.[10]

Segregation might be described as a passageway to modernity and participation, a passageway which provides both a basis of security and resources as one moves through it and a place to which one can return if need be; the more the Jews move away spatially from the ghetto, notes Louis Wirth, for example, the more they move, in religious terms, from orthodoxy to conservatism, and then to Reform. Moreover, this theme of a passageway and of transition finds its emblematic expression in the figure of the Jew, as described by Georg Simmel in his powerful article on 'the stranger' or as developed by Robert Park when he writes of the 'marginal man' – a figure described in positive terms who forms the optimistic pendant to the anti-semitic myth we encountered in the Orléans rumour.[11] Here, however, the question of racism is barely present. So-called 'ethnic' segregation, that is, the inscription in space of communities defined in predominantly cultural terms, constitutes a model which might be termed pluralistic, a model which does not exclude inter-communal tensions or even violence, but which accords each group, so long as it remains defined in cultural terms, comparable participation in social and political life. This segregation also seems to form part of a cycle which, as we have already seen in Robert Park's writings, passes through stages of contact, competition, accommodation, assimilation and amalgamation. Other authors present these stages in slightly different terms: Emory S. Bogardus, for example, notes that relations between whites and Chinese, Japanese, Filipinos or Mexicans in California move through seven phases which he lists as 'curiosity and sympathy, economic welcome, industrial and social antagonism, legislative antagonism, fair-play tendencies, quiescence and, lastly, second-generation difficulties'.[12]

Everything changes when a group begins to be treated in racial terms; segregation then assumes a quite different character.

2. Racial segregation

In the 1930s and 1940s, American sociology, including the Chicago school, became aware that the segregation of blacks, particularly in the large northern industrial cities, was not conforming to the same processes as the segregation of other minorities. The migratory movement which furnished these cities with a black proletariat 'does not conform', as René Duchac writes in an illuminating work of synthesis, 'to the same laws as the integration of white immigrant groups and even tends to develop in contrary directions',[13] and an enormous body of literature has since been devoted to explaining the specificity of a segregation which has become racial in character.

That segregation does not lead to participation in mainstream society, but ends, rather, in residential separation after a process which has four main stages that have been described – most notably by the Duncans – as follows: penetration (some blacks arrive in a white zone), invasion, consolidation and piling up.[14] The idea of a 'critical threshold' appears here, as that empirical point at which the percentage of blacks in the total population inevitably brings about segregation. This is a threshold not of tolerance, but of intolerance, which is not an expression of particular problems of integration or co-habitation, but the – racist – rejection of these. A number of studies have attempted to put a figure on this threshold: Otis Duncan, writing in the 1960s, observes that, so long as they represent less than 10 per cent of the population, blacks can generally disperse within the urban community, but beyond this figure a mechanism of segregation inescapably comes into play.[15]

Not only does racial segregation develop but it seems to supplant ethnic segregation, which declines substantially, as Karl E. Teuber and Stanley

Lieberson point out in the 1960s;[16] the principal distinction then becomes
that between white and black neighbourhoods, which is much more
marked than any between the various white neighbourhoods.

In the 1940s and 1950s, black neighbourhoods showed characteristics
which were, in many respects, comparable with those of the ethnic
minority neighbourhoods and it was possible to refer to them as black
ghettos – as did St Clair Drake and Horace R. Cayton in their book on the
'Black Metropolis' of Chicago.[17] The concentration of blacks in segregated
spaces, deserted by whites, can be explained, to a large extent, by racism,
though, contrary to received opinion, this does not necessarily imply the
collapse of the housing market.[18] Racism also accounts, to a large extent,
for the discrimination against blacks in the job market in the classic
industrial era – when they mainly occupied non-skilled, low-waged jobs –
and their *de facto* exclusion, up to the 1960s, from local and national
political life. But a moment comes when a primarily racial segregation is
reinforced – and even carried further – by other, social and economic logics
in which, in huge pockets of poverty, a black sub-proletariat forms whose
fate is no longer so explicable in terms of racism alone: hence the
provocative title of William J. Wilson's highly controversial book *The
Declining Significance of Race*.[19] Racial segregation, indissociable here
from discrimination, does not disappear, but it has built a situation – the
poverty-stricken black ghetto – which represents a legacy that, subsequently, no longer needs racism to perpetuate itself and reinforce poverty
and exclusion.

3. Total segregation

Today's black ghetto – Loïc Wacquant and William Wilson's 'hyperghetto'[20] – no longer has anything in common with Louis Wirth's classic
model. It is an area, often impressive in size, characterized by growing
poverty, sub-standard housing and inferior schooling. We cannot speak
here of culture or community: this is a space characterized, rather, by
unemployment, economic exclusion and the incapacity of its inhabitants to
mobilize resources which gave, if only perhaps to some of them, chances of
upward mobility in American society. The hyperghetto also means the
break-up of the – now frequently single-parent – family, a scarcity of
employment in the locality, and an absence of collective action outside
gangs; it is a jungle where violence and drugs quickly take over; a
combination of spatial segregation and social and economic exclusion; the
site of the formation and reproduction of a black, urban sub-proletariat,
the 'underclass' – the use of this term, which has developed in recent years,
referring to a concept some way removed from that of reserve army or
Lumpenproletariat.

The formation of this underclass would not have been possible without
the prior accumulation of various forms of racial discrimination and
segregation; but it owes a great deal – more and more, in fact – to the

transformation of the American economy and the formidable process of dualization which has been evident since the 1970s.[21] This dualization has occurred primarily in the labour market and has been effected on bases which are not racial. If the poorest, least well-trained and most deprived blacks find themselves excluded or marginalized while a very small minority of others belong to the middle strata or to that 'black bourgeoisie' which Frazier described as early as the 1950s,[22] this is because the general evolution of the economic system rejects them – not as blacks, but because they are not educated or skilled, or are too trapped in their ghettos to be aware of the job opportunities available outside or physically to have access to them. The problem is not that the whites dominate, exploit or segregate them, but lies, rather, beyond this in a situation which has become self-perpetuating, and in the general changes which are turning America into a post-industrial society.

This point, and the analysis here in general, are not accepted by everyone in the field and there have been lively controversies between two lines of thought in particular. Some hold to the view that racism is central and that this is also the case in the formation of the black 'underclass', and argue that a black sub-proletariat, which is prey to a total – social and racial – segregation, should not be over-hastily set over against black middle strata or a black bourgeoisie, whose members, they contend, also suffer racism. This was a position taken up – most prominently by Kenneth B. Clark – in the polemic triggered by the appearance of Wilson's book, to which we have already referred.[23] Others, by contrast, including Wilson himself, maintain that there is a structural division between blacks, some of whom could be said to have benefited from the advances gained in the civil rights struggles and the pressure exerted by black movements in the 1960s and 1970s and, subsequently, from 'affirmative action' programmes and quotas for minorities in employment and the universities, whereas, they argue, poor or under-educated blacks have sunk into a spiral of deprivation. It seems, overall, that this latter analysis is tending to win out and, indeed, the American Association of Black Sociologists, which was violently hostile to Wilson's arguments in the late 1970s, awarded him its highest distinction twelve years later.[24]

4. From the market to political action and the institutionalization of racism

American experience since the 1920s suggests, then, that we should initially be very cautious where the question of racial segregation is concerned. This latter is not a changeless phenomenon and it must not be confused with other logics.[25]

But we have so far only come at one aspect of the problem, which we have restricted, in the main, to processes connected predominantly with the free operation of the housing market. So long as racial segregation operates by way of a market, it has to be analysed as a set of individual behaviours informed by affects, prejudices and representations which, where racism is concerned, are widely enough shared to constitute a general orientation of action. It is indeed in this area that the phenomenon offers the most favourable terrain for an approach in terms of rational choice and maximization of advantage. A fine illustration of this approach, with reference to Great Britain, is to be found in the work of Michael Banton and also in John Rex's analyses of how segregation is very largely determined by positions in the housing market.[26]

But access to housing is not always – or not exclusively – gained by way of a private market; to a degree which varies from one society to another, public institutions – municipal, regional and national – are also involved; and that access is determined, to a greater or less extent, by specific urban and land-use policies. More generally, racial segregation is not limited to housing *in the strict sense*; it also operates around schooling, this being a focus of debate and conflict whenever the question of racism emerges and takes on clear shape within a society; and, most importantly, it is not always content to use the opportunities afforded it by the market.

Where it goes beyond these, racism begets institutionalization, that is, laws, regulations, the intervention of the public authorities and political formulation; in the contemporary world, the most spectacular instance of this has been provided by South African apartheid in the years since 1948. The transition from fragmented action on a market to a political – and indeed state – crystallization of racial segregation is achieved only by undertaking collective action in which racism is necessarily very explicit. Such action can come about in extremely varied ways. In certain cases, the political pressure is produced by a dislocation of previous social relations: in the last quarter of the nineteenth century, it was the 'poor whites' of the southern states of the USA, often under the aegis of the Farmers' Alliance, who, frightened at the prospect of blacks competing with them in the mines or the cotton fields, called most insistently for the measures which established racial segregation in public places (railroads, buses, etc.) – measures which several states were to enshrine in legislation with the 'Jim Crow' laws (Florida in 1887, Mississippi in 1888 and Texas in 1889, Louisiana in 1890, Alabama, Arkansas, Georgia and Kentucky in 1891). In other cases, segregation became institutionalized as a product of more complex processes in which social pressures mingled with other significations that were communal or, for example, nationalist in inspiration to produce a programme which might itself evolve over time, as can be seen from the history of apartheid and the successive measures taken to refine and reinforce it over forty years before its structures were dismantled at the end of the 1980s.[27]

The main point is that, in these cases, racism no longer appears merely as a factor of individual mobilization, as an orientation of the behaviour of agents in a market, but as a central signification, advanced by a political force, by movements or parties with access to state power or sufficiently influential to force it to move in a direction of their choosing. When it occurs, this leap from a diffuse racism to collective action may be more than just a continuation of spontaneous tendencies; it may generate a new dynamic – a radicalization of racism, its extension and generalization. Thus, for example, in 1948 apartheid was a slogan and a programme; by the beginning of the 1960s it had emerged as a 'unified theory', with the South African Prime Minister, Verwoerd, as its chief spokesman.[28] The early 1970s saw its embodiment in laws which excluded blacks from citizenship and the development of the homelands policy, with massive programmes of forced resettlement of the black population.

In the dynamic which the institutionalization of segregation allows to develop, violence occupies a place it can scarcely command so long as the phenomenon is located within a market. Diffuse racial segregation comes about without major acts of coercion; it seems to build up spontaneously, through the arrival and departure of individuals who, after a certain time, create a *de facto* situation of segregation. When segregation raises itself to the political level, however, it calls on para-state and even state violence to assert, maintain and extend itself. Here again, South Africa has provided what have often been dramatic images of this process, particularly in the bloody repression of the Soweto riots of 1976-7. In this regard also, racism's accession to the level of the political system and the state represents a considerable leap.

2. Racial discrimination

Racial discrimination occurs in a great number of fields, which sometimes overlap with those in which segregation (which may arise as a consequence of that discrimination) occurs. Thus, for example, by refusing to let out flats to members of a racialized group or by imposing restrictions which discourage them – making them pay more for equal quality, directing them towards some channels rather than others – the actors that sell and let – private individuals, estate agents, social housing agencies, municipal authorities, etc. – may, in fact, very well adopt a discriminatory attitude which will lead to a state of effective segregation.

Discrimination at school may also have this kind of result. By allowing the children of the racialized group to be oriented towards a school which is not necessarily segregated, but simply less effective or less well adapted to their specific difficulties, by offering them a poor quality of schooling, they are being given a future which is also more difficult, with very little chance of upward mobility, access to the best jobs or even, simply, employment information; in this way, they are marginalized or excluded.[29]

We might here, following the practice of the United Nations and the lists it issues, continue with an inventory of the places where racial discrimination might be observed.[30] It is encountered, for example, in the universities, with the quota principle; in employment, even if it seems contrary to economic logic which requires an employer to give priority to criteria which are other than racial; in trade unionism and at work, where it retards the careers and promotion of those affected;[31] in the police, which treats the members of the racialized groups differently (illegal arrests, arbitrary detention, greater use of violence against these groups); or in the legal system, as is illustrated by the copious literature in this field which shows the different sentences handed down to blacks and whites in the USA for comparable crimes[32] or which finds that, depending on whether it is carried out by whites or blacks, deviant behaviour – alcoholism, juvenile delinquency – leads, in the one case, to avenues of rehabilitation and, in the other, to much more repressive institutions.[33] The press may also be responsible for racial discrimination, only showing the racialized group in a certain light – writing only of its crimes and misdeeds, for example – or discrimination may be perpetrated by advertising which presents an alienated image of that group – that of the Uncle Tom type of 'good black' extolling the merits of a particular brand of rice or, in more modern form, of the agile, but also highly animalized black, weaving his way through the traffic jams (and the city) on his bicycle to vaunt the performance of a particular car which is able to emulate him, etc.

What is striking when we list these different fields (non-exhaustively) is the generally institutional character of racial discrimination. But institutionalization, here, does not necessarily mean that racism is declared, that it is present in the consciousness of people who at times seem more like agents than actors.

1. Institutional racism

This is why, since the late 1960s, the notion of institutional racism has been developed, one of the first – very militant – formulations of which was inseparably linked to the rise of the black movements in the USA. Racism, as Stokely Carmichael and Charles Hamilton explain,[34] can be expressed in two possible forms: it may be overt and individual or covert and institutional. The former is explicit; the latter does not need to be, and, in this case, racism does not need to appear intentional. It becomes implanted in routine practices and the functioning of organizations. Within this perspective, racism constitutes a structural property of the system and becomes, to use Blauner's expression, an 'objective phenomenon', localized in domination and the social hierarchy.[35]

This image of discrimination anchored at the institutional level refers us on, still very superficially, to a line of reasoning which stresses the idea of a system of discrimination, an integrated, inescapable machinery. Whitney Young provides a fine description of a closed loop of this kind:

> I go to the employer and ask him to employ Negroes, and he says, 'It's a matter of education. I would hire your people if they were educated.' Then I go to the educators and they say, 'If Negro people lived in good neighbourhoods and had more intelligent dialogue in their families, more encyclopaedias in their homes, more opportunity to travel, and a stronger family life, then we could do a better job of educating them.' And when I go to the builder he says, 'If they had the

money, I would sell them the houses' – and I'm back at the employer's door again, where I started to begin with.[36]

In this generalized system of discrimination, two areas of activity play a particularly crucial role: housing, since place of residence determines which school is attended, as well as access to the job market and the various spirals of drugs, violence or poverty; and schooling, since everything follows from a sub-standard education – low wages, unemployment, poor housing, etc. This conception of racism implies the existence of a vicious circle (an idea formulated by Myrdal in the 1940s), a mechanical form of operation which ensures the consolidated reproduction of the system.

This idea was taken to its extreme by Robert Friedman, who proposed that we should look not at individuals but at the forces which co-ordinate and direct their activities. American racism, explains Friedman, operates on four levels. It is, first of all, *structural*, that is, inscribed in the social structure; *procedural*, that is, transcribed into policies and procedures; *systemic*, that is, it appears in various sectors which, between them, constitute a system (housing, education, etc.); and, lastly, *ideological*, that is, expressed through representations which are often false or erroneous. From this point of view, discrimination is not connected with prejudice, nor facts with consciousness and practices with the will. 'Racism', asserts Friedman,

> may be overt or covert, conscious or unconscious, intentional or unintentional, attitudinal or behavioral. It may be the result of malice or the best of intentions; it may be based on the direct apprehension of the race of a person or group, or it may be based on criteria only peripherally related to race; it may be the result of no more than apathy, ignorance, and inertia. And it is a phenomenon distinct from prejudice which denotes negative racial attitudes.[37]

But, if it is true that racial discrimination is essentially an institutional phenomenon, how far can we go in accepting analyses which dissociate the actor from the system in this way?

2. A system without actors?

Friedman's arguments are radical and typical of a structuralism which preserves a continuity with Parsonian functionalism, attempting to subsume 'Parsons' four categories of roles, collectivities, institutions and values'.[38] In other variants, the argument is dominated, rather, by a certain ultra-leftism, with the idea that American or British society – the notion of institutional racism very soon gained a wide currency in the United Kingdom – is organized around a primary and fundamental division between whites and blacks and that racism is such a well-established system that one cannot imagine it disappearing, except by a total break, which will in fact be violent and revolutionary in nature. The structuralism, here, often takes on a Marxist coloration, in forms which are still today very vital in Britain, and, in this case, the research is directed particularly at the role of the state in the reproduction of situations structured by race.[39] In order to bring out the distinction between behaviour and prejudice and assert the primacy of structure over subjectivity, a number of writers have even proposed that this distinction be registered at the terminological level. Thus, for example, Ambalavaner Sivanandan differentiates between what he calls 'racism', an explicit ideology of racial superiority, and 'racialism', which is the unequal treatment of different races. This distinction is unstable in its content if one follows the writings of this author over time, but he always maintains it in principle.[40]

The idea of a dissociation between actor and system is not the exclusive preserve of the most radical structuralism. It may be hinted at or presented in a much more nuanced fashion, as, for instance, when a discrepancy between ideas and practices or between prejudices and discriminatory behaviour is observed. Thus, for example, Robert Merton has proposed that a distinction be made between four types (all-weather liberals, fair-weather liberals, all-weather illiberals and fair-weather illiberals), precisely to take account of the possible, but non-necessary link between discrimination and prejudice.[41]

A dissociation of this kind may also be based on a critique of the notion of prejudice, a critique eloquently formulated in the writings of David T. Wellman.[42] To speak of prejudice, explains Wellman – who, in his book, presents a number of fascinating interviews conducted with white 'racists' – is to view racism as a combination of hostility towards and false generalizations about groups defined by race. But how, for example, are we to react to whites who, without expressing the least anti-black prejudice, simply wish to maintain a status quo which operates to their advantage and who reject calls for institutional change coming from the black population? What are we to think of those who oppose educational segregation but reject compulsory busing because it forces their children to spend too much time travelling? Wellman finds that those who choose to conceive of racism merely as prejudice – and who consider it sufficient to behave in a rational manner, conforming to the American ideals of egalitarianism, not to be thought a racist – do not see racism as it exists in its concrete manifestations. And he denounces this position, which is, in his view, merely an ideology of the right-thinking, white middle classes, raised on the values of Myrdal's American creed. Moreover, notes Wellman, the middle classes cannot see that the 'racism = prejudice' equation is a luxury they afford themselves which allows them to treat racism as a form of deviance verging on personality disorder, but does not prevent them from developing racist sentiments as soon as they are directly affected by the demands and behaviour of blacks.

In fact, the practice of institutional discrimination is never totally masked from – or invisible to – those who gain by it. By virtue of the debates it generates, the investigations and reports to which it gives rise, the collective action of those who reject it (not all of whom are necessarily members of the groups discriminated against), the intervention of intellectuals or religious leaders and the mediation of the press, it situates racism at a level which continues to be affected by pressure or resistance from those who suffer the discrimination. This is, incidentally, one of the most interesting aspects of British anti-racism legislation, which, in the 1976 Act, recognizes the notion of 'indirect discrimination' – a notion closely related to that of institutional racism – and provides the Commission for Racial Equality with the means to carry out studies into this particular form of racism.[43]

However, taken to its logical conclusions, the idea of an institutional racism split off from the consciousness of its agents leads to an unacceptable paradox, since it implies that the whole of the dominant group is both totally innocent and totally guilty. It exonerates everyone, since the system alone is responsible; it indicts everyone, since everyone derives benefit from it and participates in it. This is an untenable position. Would it have been possible, for example, at the end of the Second World War, when the high dignitaries of the Nazi regime were arrested and brought before the tribunals, to accept their protestations that they had not been responsible for what had happened? Can we believe that all those in Poland who say they were merely passive witnesses to the destruction of the Jews in Europe were merely indifferent bystanders? Do we not, rather, have to make a distinction between those who were, to varying degrees, revolted but impotent and those who, more or less confusedly, found that destruction a source of satisfaction – a phenomenon strikingly illustrated in Claude Lanzmann's film *Shoah*?

Precisely because it is, to a large extent, a form of institutionalization of racism, discrimination functions at a level which is not that of the production of the phenomenon. It is not the direct, immediate transcription of representations and perceptions of the Other and of prejudices, but, rather, an expression distanced from it to a greater or lesser degree, a set of practices which have acquired a certain autonomy and a dynamic of their own, but a dynamic which is shaped by contradictory affects and interests arising out of history and the work of society on itself.

Unlike racial segregation and its extreme variant, the extermination or expulsion of the racialized group, racial discrimination incorporates that group, but does so in a mode which renders it inferior. It does not set up a project of separation, or indeed of breaking with or destroying that other group, but forms a part of the social and political relations with it. It does not, in itself, constitute a mobilizing force – or at least nothing so powerful as the force which drives programmes of segregation. Hence the further paradox that, by institutionalizing itself, it is able partially to elude the consciousness of the actors and, at the same time, become an integral part of various fields of social life. As a force of rupture, exclusion or destruction, when it raises itself to the political level, segregation-based racism acquires a legitimacy in the eyes of the actor which makes it easy consciously to espouse it as a credo. By contrast, discrimination-based racism, being an instrument – but also a perversion – of relations of domination, being associated with collective advantage – or with the dream or phantasy of such advantage – and being anchored in institutions, continues to be shaped by social demands, by conflict and by phenomena of upward or – more importantly – downward mobility. But it is the less conscious or perceived and the less associated with prejudice in that it is possible to present or experience it, with a greater or lesser degree of bad faith, as something other than racism – for example, as the defence of economic interest or social position. Thus, when segregation reaches the political level, this involves mobilization and awareness on the part of the actors. On the other hand, when discrimination penetrates into the institutional system, practice tends to become dissociated from prejudice, and action from consciousness – or such a dissociation at least becomes possible.

8

RACIST VIOLENCE

If, in Serge Moscovici's fine formulation, there is a 'hard core' of racism, 'a tangible, resistant material around which one may circle as electrons circle around their nucleus, but into which one cannot penetrate',[1] then surely this is to be found in the violence it permits or provides a basis for – the massacres, lynchings, pogroms, killings and attacks, to say nothing of the more minor persecutions such as threats, anonymous letters and limited forms of aggression. Efforts have been made, from time to time, to build up a unified picture of the process which leads to racist violence. Gordon W. Allport, for example, says that he 'can be fairly certain' that when such violence breaks out, a series of steps have prepared the way for it. He gives a nine-point list of these: a long period in which the victim group has been subject to prejudices in which it is categorized racially; a long period, too, in which the habit of complaining about that group, of blaming it and suspecting it, has become firmly rooted; growing discrimination; increased strain and privation; irrationalism has developed a strong appeal and exasperation verges on a state of explosion; individuals have been attracted by organized movements or by less formal organizations such as a mob; individuals have derived courage or support from such organizations, feeling their actions justified by the standards of the group; an incident occurs or is invented, the invention circulating as a rumour; a 'social facilitation' effect has been produced by the first violent acts.[2]

When the process of the lifting of the restraints which prevent verbal aggression from developing into outright violence is formulated in this way, the implication is that these forms are located on a continuum. This is a point worthy of discussion. The suggestion is, for example, that racism is from the outset the driving force behind the action. This is not, however, necessarily the case: as we have observed in studies conducted on the subject of terrorism, even if it was perhaps present embryonically or secondarily in their initial ideology, the anti-semitism of some of the most radical Palestinian or Armenian groups is more the product of their final drift into an aggravated form of terrorism than the starting point for their actions.[3] This is why, rather than asserting the deep unity or continuity of the phenomenon which ends in racist violence, it seems preferable to keep to the principle of an analytic approach, based in this case on three main elements. The first is the idea that such violence is not necessarily the outcome of a single mechanism and that not one, but several modes of reasoning are required to account for it, and these may have to be combined to explain its most complex manifestations. The second concerns what is, in our view, the crucial distinction between the political and institutional expressions of racist violence, on the one hand, and those expressions which are not – or not yet – political or institutional. The third and last element relates to the limited or unlimited character of the violence, as observed in the gravest historical experiences, such as Nazism or apartheid.

1. Approaches to violence

There are a number of major paradigms in the general sociology of violence and these can be applied to the more specific case of racism.[4]

The most frequently applied regards violent behaviour as the mark or consequence of social or political crisis (or disorganization). There are several variants within this general perspective. Some writers stress the loss or weakening of control, which releases affects, impulses and more or less instinctive tendencies to aggression, particularly in crowds. In a tradition which runs, with many nuances, from Gustave Le Bon to Sigmund Freud, via Gabriel Tarde and Scipio Sighele, crowds are regarded as emotive, suggestive, boundlessly credulous, intransigent, radical, unable to distinguish between ideas and acts, and amenable to appeals which present them with a scapegoat; the crowd 'believes it has discovered that some group or other, perhaps the Jews or the blacks, is threatening it', explains Serge Moscovici. 'It ascribes imaginary crimes to them – ritual murders or rape for example – and eventually organises pogroms or lynchings.'[5]

A somewhat different variant concerns itself not so much with crowds as with the masses, or, more precisely, with the massification of modern societies which, in becoming urbanized, lose their structures and earlier forms of organization. The destruction of community and intermediate groups, explains William Kornhauser, for example, prepares the ground for extreme behaviour and totalitarianism. The atomization of the social body and the space this opens up for mass politics then begets violence, including racist violence.[6]

Even further removed from crowd analysis, there is a third variant of the crisis behaviour approach, in terms either of the most classical functionalism or, most significantly, of a neo-functionalism which finds its highest expression in the work of Ted Robert Gurr. Here, violence is seen as expressing the relative frustration of an actor who has been thwarted in his aspirations and becomes aggressive as a consequence. It conforms to a psychological dynamic valid for all civil violence throughout the world:

> American Negro rioters and their white antagonists seem to share one basic psychological dynamic with striking French farmers, Guatemalan guerillas, and rioting Indonesian students: most of them feel frustrated in the pursuit of their goals, they are angered as a consequence, and because of their immediate social circumstances they feel free enough, or desperate enough, to act on that anger.[7]

This vast range of analyses has the virtue of emphasizing the conditions within the social system which encourage the expression of racism. It is also open to a number of criticisms which distinctly limit its significance. However, we shall leave these aside for the moment and move on to examine two other types of argument which are centred much more on the calculations and the meaning violence brings into play.[8]

The first of these perspectives sees violence as a form of instrumental action governed by the interests, if not indeed the calculations, of the participants. This is a utilitarian point of view which is also at the heart of the rational choice theories and suggests that violence is linked to the hope of gain on the part of its perpetrators. If, for example, the white populations of the great northern cities of the USA murder a great many blacks during rioting, as happened in Chicago in 1919 and in East St Louis in 1917, then, according to this approach, this is an attempt to interrupt the massive influx of blacks and the unrestrained competition they introduce into the labour and housing markets. If, in the immediate post-war period, Poland is rocked by pogroms, this is an attempt to drive away the few Jews who had gone there to rebuild their lives or even to recover their property, etc. Racist violence, for this type of approach, can be analysed in individual terms, as if the participants might find personal satisfaction of either a material or symbolic nature in it. It can also be analysed in collective and political terms, within the tradition of the sociology of resource mobilization, for example, by way of the idea that such violence may enable the victimized group to be expelled from a system of political participation or from its economic positions. Here, racist violence is seen as a means to certain ends.

Once again, however, this has only a weak explanatory value. Who would dare, for example, to reduce the Nazi experience to the instrumental action of a clique, party or population? Just because the means are appropriate to the ends and the behaviour is therefore rational – as is attested, in the Nazi case, by the remarkable material organization of the final solution[9] – we cannot take it that the violence itself always has to be understood as a mere means. In almost every case, its meaning far exceeds the notion of instrumentality: it has to do with the subjectivity of actors, and not just their calculations and interests; it relates to orientations of action, not just to individual and collective strategies. In this latter perspective, violence is the outcome of a management of significations comparable, in principle, to what we advanced in Chapter 6 with regard to the prejudice that is linked with differentialist racism. Not because it transcribes this directly into action, nor because it is, necessarily, a continuation of it, but because it attests to the existence of the same type of processes, which are processes of the loss and reconstitution of meaning.

From this point of view, racist violence represents a mode of resolution of tensions in which these are taken out on a scapegoat in the wake – and this is the key point – of a loss of social and cultural bearings, or a threat to those bearings, or a de-structuring of social, political or community

relations, or the – real or imagined – risk of such a de-structuring.
Prejudice is a soft form of this process, or one that is moderated by the
state of the political system and the state. Violence is its radical,
unadulterated form, when political or moral constraints are weak or
weakened, when the political authorities are themselves won over to this
process, or tolerant of it.

In its concrete expressions, racist violence is an historical phenomenon
and, as such, is always a product of a great many causes or factors, making
each of these expressions unique events, even if they are reproduced in an
identical form – like the pogroms of central Europe at the turn of the
century or the lynchings in the southern states of the USA which were so
numerous and repetitive between 1890 and 1920. Each of these events
represents a synthesis, the various elements of which may very well be
explicable in terms of the different approaches to which we have just
rapidly alluded, or others we have not mentioned. This is why we should
not set these various approaches up in opposition to one another, but
rather examine, with each case of racist violence we consider, whether –
and to what extent – they bring some explanatory power to bear. But if we
are seeking, in a particular experience, to isolate a pure element which is
more especially indicative of the racist character of the violence, then it
seems to us that it has to be sought either in the processes of loss of
meaning, which cause an imaginary representation to lead an actor to grant
himself permission to attack the social and physical existence of the Other,
or in what it is that violence contributes, in a more or less instrumental
way, to maintaining a racial order and domination.

2. Three levels

Racist violence, however minor or fragmented it may seem, is never totally
independent of the political context in which it arises. But we should make
an analytical distinction here between three very different levels. Violence
is, in fact, always informed or conditioned by the state of the political
system or by the state, but it may intervene at another level; it may also
itself become political, that is, be taken in hand by more or less organized
forces which place it at the centre of a project and action which are directly
political. It may, lastly, be institutionalized in a state and constitute a
central principle of its functioning.

The demarcation lines between these three types of phenomena are not
always clearly drawn and many experiences are of an intermediate
character or oscillate between two levels. We must, none the less, establish
these demarcation lines theoretically and, indeed, must do so firmly. When
it is infra-political, racist violence seems impulsive, spontaneous and
fragmented, and appears to spring up in particular conjunctures in which
social and political controls are relaxed, namely where state order is distant
or absent, in fluid situations, in the form of crowd phenomena or even of

rioting. The picture it presents is one of the explosion, aggravation and sudden resolution of quasi-instinctual, unpremeditated tensions. By contrast, political racial violence seems ideologically structured, organized and prepared; it is directed, channelled, controlled and self-controlled, impelled by agents who shape it more or less expertly. This is also the image presented by state violence, which, though it may be quite frenzied, can none the less appear cold and bureaucratic. Racist violence, to invoke a classical, but superficial, distinction, seems the more instrumental the more it takes the form of political or state violence and the more expressive the more it takes an infra-political form. The transition from one level to the other does not always occur and is not necessarily clear-cut; but, where it does occur, it represents a substantial break. Thus, for example, an important turning point in the history of Nazism occurred in November 1938, when, following the anti-semitic violence of *Kristallnacht* – orchestrated by Goebbels but involving broad sections of the population – the regime decided to exert much stricter control on anti-semitic practices. It assumed a legal monopoly over these and directed them towards much more methodical ends, though it did so by measures somewhat removed from popular expectations or emotions.[10]

There is a scale that runs from acts of quasi-isolated violence which are not political in character to state measures which are controlled and even, in the case of Nazism, turned – if only partially – into state secrets (the 'terrible secret' Walter Laqueur writes of).[11] We shall attempt to show the gradations of that scale, which merely further refines the main distinction between two levels, the political and the infra-political – levels we have already qualified above by dividing the political level into the two sub-sets of party system and state.

(a) At the furthest remove from the state and the political system, racist violence may arise, in spite of moral and political prohibitions, in highly localized situations. These may occur in places of transit, where all control is absent (such as deserted trains at night, tube stations), or a particular tension may arise (as when some incident occurs, such as a brawl in a bar or outside a night-club). Even in these cases, it is exceptional for the violence to be caused by a single actor, and, when this is the case, as for example when a shopkeeper fires off his gun in an isolated act, there is generally a basis for the action in a legitimacy provided by other people in the immediate environment or by the dissemination of a theme such as the fear of crime [*l'insécurité*].

(b) Racist violence may also be linked to a local weakening or erosion of state or political control. Allen D. Grimshaw provides some illustrations of this phenomenon which relate to the US race riots of the early years of this century.[12] Though clearly it cannot be attributed solely to this factor, the violence which occurred at Springfield in 1908, East St Louis in 1917 and Chicago in 1919 none the less took place against a background of corruption within the municipal authorities. A state that is too distant, or a 'frontier' situation, also open up a space where, in the name of order, a violence occurs which may, in fact, resemble established, legal forms, when there is recourse to what is known as 'lynch law' after the Justice of the Peace who held trials in his own house and summarily condemned horse thieves to forty lashes, meted out to them on the spot. Another form of the slackening of state control is seen when the state becomes unable to some degree to prevent certain police practices in which a discrimination that is more or less an established part of the police's style of working deteriorates into physical violence. Thus, for example, Jean-Claude Monet has suggested that, in the case of France, a number of police 'errors', which are to all intents and purposes racist crimes, are not so much products of the racist prejudices with which the French police is seriously imbued as 'professional dysfunctions' which result from the

> police officer's incapacity to structure a fluctuating, ambiguous or equivocal situation other than by recourse to impoverished and stereotyped patterns of action. The classic scenario is that of the night-time identity check, unobserved by anyone outside the police force, which ends in an officer opening fire impulsively; or the attempt to intercept a vehicle for a routine road traffic offence which turns into a – possibly lethal – car-chase.[13]

(c) Before becoming entrenched at state level, racist violence may elevate itself to the level of the political system and may then accompany an action or pressures sanctioned by political or moral forces. Thus, in post-war Poland, for example, it is not possible to understand the many anti-semitic attacks – which lasted until 1947 and culminated in the Kielce pogrom (4 July 1946) in which 42 Jews were massacred – if one does not take into account the general attitude of the Catholic church and most of the Polish political Right who linked their hatred of the Jews who had survived the war and remained in – or returned to – Poland with their detestation of the Communist regime which was then establishing itself and extending its hold over the country.[14] We are here approaching a first demarcation line which separates infra-political from political violence, insofar as there is a great ideological proximity between crowds involved in pogroms and forces which intervene at the political level: we are even astride that line here to the extent that an episode such as that at Kielce necessarily involves ringleaders and agitators who are more or less connected with such forces. We do not really cross it, however, at least so long as no genuine link is established between the action and an organized party or group.

(d) A genuine leap across that line occurs at the point when the violence is structured, when it is written into the programme or project of one or more established forces and given a certain stability over time. Racism may be at the heart of the action here, as it is for the American Ku Klux Klan and similar organizations. It may also be only a secondary element or one whose importance and thematics vary as the movement develops. For instance, the groups of skinheads, which first appeared in Britain in the late 1960s, have come more and more distinctly to assert not just an anti-black and anti-Asian racism, but a growing anti-semitism which is neo-Nazi in

inspiration. Violence, at this stage, may be carried out by secret organizations or by clandestine offshoots, the armed wings of movements with
official identities which operate within legal or legitimate forms and whose
racism is presented in a cautious and carefully toned-down manner. It may,
in this case, be only poorly controlled by the legal – or most central –
movement or party, and may even become independent of it and,
conceivably, appear to act in a way that runs counter to its political or
strategic orientations.

Thus, Palestinian-inspired terrorism takes on an increasingly anti-semitic
– rather than merely anti-Zionist or anti-Israeli – coloration the further one
moves from Fatah, the most central organization of the PLO. And, in quite
a different register, the racist attacks carried out by the contemporary
extreme Right in France seem to run counter to the legalist strategy of the
Front national – which does not necessarily mean that the racist violence of
the one group can be entirely dissociated from the political project of the
other.

(e) Lastly, a second decisive step is taken at the point when, in one way
or another, racist violence is recognized, accepted and orchestrated by the
government of the state. We should distinguish here between at least three
different types of such violence. Racism may be an instrument employed
by a crisis-stricken or weakened regime to disguise its own impotence or its
difficulties, which are then imputed to a *scapegoat*. This was a regular
practice under the last Russian Czars, for example, where discrimination
against the Jews, their segregation, the spreading – chiefly by the political
police, the Okhrana – of a propaganda of which the *Protocols of the Elders
of Zion* is merely one example, and the manipulation of popular anti-
semitism were all combined in an effort aimed mainly at concealing
military failures, or lessening their impact. The great historian Simon
Dubnow provides a fine description of how, between 1880 and 1915,
responsibility for the ills which struck Russia was always in the end placed
at the door of the Jews. They were excluded from a wide range of
economic activities, were subject to quota systems in both the grammar
schools and the universities, could live only in the outer regions of the
country and were virtually banned from a great many towns and forced,
into the bargain, to perform lengthy military service. Thus, as a result of
the watchword 'Find the Jew!' which went out in 1881 after the assassination of Alexander II, they bore the bitter brunt of the counter-revolution
of 1905. And, in wartime, the army and the government not only organized
anti-semitic propaganda, but also issued calls to carry out pogroms, when
they were not in fact very concretely preparing them themselves. 'Germans
and Yids, they're all the same, they're all traitors. The commander said
so,' explained Russian soldiers in 1914 to a Jewish member of the same
army, defending the same motherland.[15]

Another type of violence is that in which the state stands as *guarantor of
a social order* functioning on the basis of a two-fold principle of discrimination and segregation. In South African apartheid, which is the most

prominent example, the problem is not one of identifying a scapegoat, but rather of using, where necessary, the state's legitimate monopoly of violence for repressive ends, in order to maintain order in police and military-style actions which border at times on terror.

A third and last type is that in which state violence does not tend to reproduce an order, but goes much further than the pursuit of a scapegoat and moves into a *purely exterminatory and destructive spiral*. The USSR under Stalin came close to this model and it would perhaps have taken hold if Stalin's death in 1953 had not interrupted a process in which the Jewish doctors' 'plot' was merely one stage;[16] clearly, however, Nazi Germany provides the main example of a process of this kind.

3. The limits of violence

Whether conditioned or permitted by the political and state system, or itself a political – or state – phenomenon, racist violence never arises in a social vacuum; it points, almost always, directly or indirectly, to social relations and changes, to phenomena of mobility and social decline, and to population movements, as well as to the constitution, reinforcement or defence of groups self-defined by their identity, by their belonging to a religious, national, ethnic and, ultimately, racial community. Which prompts us to proffer two new observations.

The first is that, when read in the light of its social and communal significations, a single form of racist violence may very well correspond to situations which extremely different but all of which resolve themselves in identical practices. Anti-black riots in the USA, like lynchings, provide a good illustration of this point. Allen Grimshaw's studies very clearly show that two types of riot exist.[17] The 'northern-style' form, which occurred in the great industrial cities of the North, correlates with anxieties and tensions stirred up by the large-scale movements of blacks from the South. They had moved not only up the country but also up the social ladder, and there was apparently nothing to halt their social ascent; hence the exasperation and growing fear on the part of the whites and the outbreaks of violence which themselves fed on a certain capacity on the part of the blacks to respond. The starting point of the Chicago riots of July 1919 is highly symbolic. Everything began, in fact, at the lakeside, where whites and blacks were separated on two different beaches and where a line, which was imaginary but none the less respected in principle, extended that separation out into the water. Some young blacks had, for their amusement, crossed the line – or so, at least, the rumour ran – and stones were thrown from the beach, killing a first victim. Back in the city, things degenerated and 38 people died.

'Southern-style' violence, by contrast, does not correlate with improvement in the position of the blacks and the beginnings of integration; its central aim is to put the 'negroes' in their place and maintain a traditional order. It inflicts terror on the victimized group, so that that group will again bend the knee and clearly demonstrate its submissiveness. This is why this southern-style violence falls away again as soon as it has expressed itself and succeeded in restoring the racial order, whereas its northern-style counterpart, resolving none of the problems from which it arises, leaves behind high levels of tension after the riots.

We must also, as a number of studies have suggested, distinguish between two types of lynching.[18] In its 'Bourbon' form, the lynching is an act carried out by prosperous, influential citizens, engaged in punishing the 'guilty party' – in general, a black accused of a crime – which is frequently the rape or attempted rape of a white woman. In this case, it is a well-ordered, 'well-mannered' event and constitutes primarily a reminder to respect the racial order in a town or region where such an order has long existed. There is, on the other hand, a popular form of lynching, which is disorderly, but also more savage and bestial, less precise in the choice of its victims and more prevalent in situations where blacks and 'poor whites' are in competition, or in periods of economic difficulty, such as are occasioned, for example, by falls in the price of cotton.[19] In both cases, the theme of sexual crime is frequently evident, probably because the sexual barrier is the ultimate taboo, the last and most important bulwark of an order or a difference (of 4,730 lynchings recorded between 1882 and 1951, where a white victim was, to some extent, involved, 25.3 per cent arose out of accusations of rape or attempted rape).

To turn now to the second comment, without it being possible to describe this as an absolute rule, racist violence is often preceded or accompanied by a rumour, which provides it with its immediate justification. Rumour is a catalytic element in pogroms or lynchings in particular and it binds the participants around a mythic narrative which condenses and displaces the tension or the concrete difficulties of the actor. Indeed, the actor gains considerable strength from it, especially when it relates to the sacred, to sex or to blood. On hundreds of occasions throughout history, anti-semitic violence has been linked to accusations of ritual crime – particularly of child-murder, as in the Beilis case, named after the Jewish worker accused of such a crime in 1911 – an accusation which served as a prelude to a massive wave of pogroms under the Czarist regime – or in the Kielce pogrom, which we have already mentioned, the pretext for which was an imaginary account of an attempt by Jews to kidnap a child.[20]

These comments bring us to a last line of questioning: is racist violence not fundamentally different depending on whether it is linked to a situation defined mainly in social terms (of inequality or discrimination), or one defined mainly in terms of community (the call for homogeneity and for the segregation or even the elimination of the racialized group), or a situation in which these two dimensions are inextricably linked? Our answer will take the form of the following hypothesis.

Where racist violence is based mainly on discrimination – whether the aim is to increase, establish or maintain it – where it is linked to an inegalitarian treatment of the racialized group and very real social relations, it remains within limits which are those of the very existence of those relations: to the extent that it is associated with rendering a group inferior, violence cannot aim to destroy or reject that group. Where, by contrast, its inclination is to exclude the group, to set it apart, it may assume the form of an unbounded phenomenon: massive terror, physical elimination of the proscribed race – the 'final solution' as the Nazis put it. Lastly, where the two phenomena are indissociably linked, violence oscillates between tendencies towards a degree of limitation and counter-vailing tendencies towards the destruction of the racialized group – tendencies it cannot totally give in to, however, unless those promoting it choose to destroy the very foundations of their domination.

In this sense, Nazism and apartheid are radically distinct historical experiences. The former became clearly oriented, very early on, towards a project of extermination of the Jews and Gypsies. The latter attempted throughout to combine segregation and discrimination and it is only with the failure of that project, at the point when apartheid is disintegrating, that a watershed is being reached and there is some danger of seeing a purely destructive violence – a splintered-off element of a de-structured model – acquire an autonomous dynamic in radicalized white minority sectors.

CONCLUSION

The analytic distinctions we have arrived at for examining the concrete manifestations of racism seem to us to operate effectively. When it can be seen as relating predominantly to an inegalitarian logic and to relations of domination, prejudice is not of the same order as when it constructs a differentialist representation of the Other directed towards setting him apart, or indeed expelling or exterminating him. Similarly, violence performs distinct functions and gives expression to different tensions depending on whether it corresponds predominantly to the one logic or the other; and depending also on whether it remains infra-political, appears at a political level or provides the guiding spirit for state action – the decisive demarcation line running between the first of these three levels and the other two. Segregation is clearly associated more with processes of differentiation, and discrimination with relations of inequality.

Racism's transition to the political level occurs in different ways, depending on whether it is a matter, on the one hand, of setting in place and ratifying a relationship of domination, transcribing that relationship into an order and then maintaining that order, or, on the other, of developing forms of racial exclusion, which may in certain cases involve taking these to the most final, most murderous extremes. In the one case, what is being pursued, legitimated or rationalized by racism is a structural equilibrium, corresponding to a racial principle of social organization; in the other, racism is a force for change which sets the racializing collectivity in motion. This is why, in the former case, racism may penetrate institutions and even shape economic and social life without collective actors necessarily having to subscribe to it and even without its most decisive agents or most immediate beneficiaries having to express any great prejudice; in the second case, by contrast, the politicization of the phenomenon is indissociable from a high degree of collective mobilization. In racism of the predominantly inegalitarian kind, it is not necessary for the Other to be visible and for domination or exploitation to show up his inferiority. It is enough that he keeps to his place, carrying out the dirty or unpleasant work; his poverty is not a source of embarrassment and his alienation is accepted – indeed, even desired – and it is easy to understand why, in this case, an important part of the protest of blacks in the USA has consisted in denouncing the invisibility of black people or their caricaturing in the 'Uncle Tom' figure. In difference-based racism, by contrast, the Other has to be identified, recognized and pointed out all the more insistently for the fact that his phenotypical particularism is totally mythical: anti-semitism in Germany developed in an historical conjuncture when the Jews were largely assimilated, participated massively in modern life and had to a very great extent abandoned the most visible attributes of their religion or their specific culture.

The two fundamental logics of racism – the inegalitarian and the differentialist – are interrelated in many historical situations. Where difference is subordinated to inequality, where segregation is materially in the service of discrimination, for example, where a society is sufficiently strong to impose a principle of the racial organization of social relations, to translate this into political terms and write it into the functioning of the state, whilst drawing sustenance from certain forms of exclusion of the dominated, racialized group, stability is greater than in the opposite case. Where, in effect, the logic of difference is combined for a time with that of inequality, but governs and shapes it, it may tend to jettison this latter logic and deny it, and go freewheeling off on a course of its own.

As we observed at the end of the first part of this work, the theoretical unity of racism cannot be inferred from an examination of the partial theories the social sciences have elaborated over more than a century. That unity seems even more problematic as we bring this second part to a close, since the elementary forms of the phenomenon not only seem very diversified but also lend themselves easily to the attempt to break them down analytically. What is worse, we do not simply move from one of these forms to another and it is impossible to offer solid arguments to explain how they are directly interrelated. In some cases, prejudice heralds, prepares or accompanies violence; in others, violence does not occur: at times, racism seems to arise out of a direct relationship of domination of the racializing over the racialized group; at others, the racialized group is very largely a mythical construct. Institutional discrimination permits of a certain dissociation between actor and system, but this is much less the case with segregation once it has been elevated to the political level. And so on. It is as though the whole range of concrete manifestations of racism derived from a single – complex – system to which we do not yet possess the keys.

We already know, however, that the analysis of racism involves our referring to the *subjectivity* of the actor and contextualizing that subjectivity in *relations* which cannot be reduced simply to race relations. We know the usefulness of the distinctions which separate the political from the infra-political level of racist action and which suggest that we should not confuse an inegalitarian logic – generally linked with relations of domination – with a differentialist one – generally linked to a *community becoming centred on itself* or to its expansion or its separating off of anything which is not homogeneous with it. In reality we are not far from our goal now. We merely have to shift the perspective once again, and, much more directly than we have so far, to consider racism as an action, and examine the conditions which make possible its emergence, extension or evolution.

PART THREE
THE UNITY OF RACISM

INTRODUCTION

An essential distinction, firmly established by Alain Touraine, requires that the analysis of collective action be organized, in general, around two basic axes.[1] The first of these concerns the relations at work within a society, whether we are looking at social movements, political pressures or organizational demands; the second relates to historical change and the behaviours which arise out of the relationships between one community and others. The study of the division of a society takes its orientation from the social axis, the study of its unity and development from the historical or communal axis.

In many respects, racism seems to sit astride these two axes. On the one hand, as we particularly saw when looking at the position of blacks in the USA, it is indissociably linked to relations of domination and is inscribed in the social structure, giving expression to one of the most important divisions within that structure. On the other hand, it plays a central role in projects of exclusion or destruction, a phenomenon seen in one of its major forms whenever anti-semitism sets out to purify or homogenize a national collectivity. But, though it is linked, on the one hand, to social action and, on the other, to historical action, it displays specific characteristics which prevent us from regarding it as belonging directly to either; it has its own logics and constitutes, in itself, a set of autonomous significations, which are capable, in extreme cases, of leading on to political projects.

Should we, then, add a third axis to the two main axes of the analysis of action and draw up a theoretical picture of a new group of behaviours? In reality, this idea does not stand up for very long, quite simply because what gives racism its originality or specificity arises largely out of – more or less distorted – elements taken from the two classical axes of action.

On the one hand, in effect, racism is, as Albert Memmi has it, 'a failure of relationship',[2] and, more precisely, of the social relation; it arises in times of weakness and crisis, times when it is not possible to construct properly social relations, to participate in such relations and make them a central principle of the organization of society. As we shall see, the scope for racism expands as the space for social conflict – particularly the space for the highest expression of those conflicts: social movements – contracts.

From this point of view, racist action constitutes a negation, and sometimes even an inversion, of social action.

On the other hand, racism always seems ready to well up from within communal movements. It is frequently present, particularly in nationalist or religious movements, as though it constituted not a negation but a potentiality of all historical action. From this point of view, its scope increases not in times of decline or weakness, but when this type of action is undergoing transformation. Lastly, racism as action may very well play on the two registers and accumulate or fuse elements of meaning which both arise out of failing social relations and derive from communal significations. We can even say that this is the most common case historically.

As a consequence, we shall here view racism as an action which finds its modalities of expression and specific field of application in the work of societies on themselves, in the social relations which form the basis of those societies and in the upsurges or diminutions of community feeling which occur within them.

9

SOCIAL MOVEMENTS AND RACISM

The more a society is organized on the basis of a social conflict properly so-called – whether one refers to such a conflict as a relation between classes [*un rapport de classe*] or speaks of a social movement – and the more that conflict is central, fuelling the engines of political life and the functioning of the state, governing the main debates within the society and the commitments of its intellectuals, the more restricted is the space for racism. Conversely, the weaker the degree of social conflict and the less such conflicts shape the political system and the state, the greater the space for racism.

A society may be not so much structured by a central social relation as stratified; in that case, it is dominated by phenomena of social mobility, at the end of which the actors, defined by their relative positions in the system, are characterized by their unequal access to consumption and culture, by their greater or lesser capacity to conform to the legitimate values which orientate action, and by behaviours of upward or downward mobility. The main groups are not then necessarily social; they may also be defined in terms of community, particularly in the case where such groups are ethnic minorities. The general integration of society, if that society is open and democratic, then takes place around political formulas which are often encapsulated in the term 'pluralism'. Social stratification is some-times so rigid, if only for certain groups, that one might be tempted to speak of a caste system. On the other hand, that stratification may present a picture of great fluidity which seems to encourage analyses that are classically liberal in inspiration or centred on market mechanisms (the labour, housing and education markets, etc.).

These brief remarks give only a very partial picture of the range of social and political situations in which racism is encountered, and, to provide a more complete account, we would have at least to mention slave-owning or colonial societies and frontier situations, among others. But they allow us to make clear our view that the more a society is marked by a fundamental division – where the dominant and dominated actors are ranged against each other in a conflictual relation in which that society's most basic orientations, its historicity and its capacity to produce material goods are at issue, along with its culture and modes of knowledge and relations with itself and with nature – the more problems of stratification, mobility and the integration of the diverse community groups which make it up or the markets in which the actors meet are over-determined by this conflictual relation, which necessarily governs the analysis – including the analysis of racism.

This is the idea, as yet only crudely formulated, which will guide our deliberations here. In what follows, we shall give it more precise theoretical expression and illustrate it with concrete examples. But let us point up at the outset the chief limitation of this approach, which relates to the fact that one can never move automatically from sociological to historical analysis. To say that there is a link between the central organizing principle of a society and the place of racism within that society is to advance a general hypothesis based on a precise category of analysis or a set of theoretically integrated categories. To test that hypothesis, or at least to illustrate it, is to apply it to experiences which do indeed enable us to validate it, but without necessarily excluding all sorts of other hypotheses. We are not in the business, then, of explaining racism in terms of a single cause (to which the historian would quite properly ask that we add others), but are intent on showing – and this is something very different – that a particular mode of analysis sheds a useful light on the understanding of certain historical realities.

Our approach will not be comparative, in the sense of considering a certain number of societies in the light of a major hypothesis which relates to their central organizing principle. It will start out from what constitutes the most decisive element of a fundamental, conflictual social relation and examine what happens, from the point of view of racism, when that element is weak or becomes de-structured. In other words, our approach will relate the highest theoretically possible expression of a social conflict – the existence of a social movement (and we shall again provide a precise definition of this) – to the modalities of formation and extension of racist discourses and practices.

The study of social movements has never taken racism as a central category of analysis. At best, we can report two main types of effort in this direction, though they are in fact very different in kind.

On the one hand, concern has been shown from time to time in the historical investigation of certain social movements, beginning with the labour movement, to describe the presence of more or less racist ideas and behaviour among the oppositional actors themselves, either in the form of more or less mass-based, but relatively sporadic violence, the clearly expressed imprint of a racist ideology or, alternatively, a sustained practice of racism, institutionalized in the forms of organization this particular social actor has adopted. Thus, for example, Pierre Milza has written about the murderous, almost riotous violence which was inflicted, in a spirit more xenophobic than racist, on Italian agricultural workers and labourers at Aigues-Mortes in the south of France in 1893; Michel Winock, again writing about France, has shown to what degree, in that same period, the workers' organizations were imbued with anti-semitism, making them more *anti-dreyfusard* than is commonly thought; and a wealth of literature documents how, again at the turn of the century, American trade unionism long excluded or discriminated against blacks – and, more briefly, Asians – particularly in California.[1]

On the other hand, the sociological, political or psycho-sociological study of certain forms of collective behaviour dominated or shaped by racism has inclined some writers to regard these as social movements. Hadley Cantril, for example, in his psychological theorization of social movements, has looked at lynchings and at Nazism, and, very recently, Birgitta Orfali, drawing at length on Cantril's work, has sought to show how the Front national in France has moved from the situation of an active minority to that of a social movement.[2] But if, following Alain Touraine, we wish to give a precise meaning to the concept of social movement,[3] and wish to see it as a form of conflictual action set within the framework of a structural relationship of domination, and carried forward by an actor able to recognize a particular social identity as his own and another as that of his adversary, and able, also, to situate himself on a terrain shared by the actor opposing him – and, therefore, capable of acting to control the same stakes and the same cultural resources – then the behaviours studied by Cantril or Orfali seem to be of a different nature. This does not, however, mean, as we shall see, that the concept of social movement does not help us to analyse them.

1. Race and class

For its part, the study of racism has often sought to relate this phenomenon to the image of a society riven by a basic conflict, contradictorily structured by relations of domination and therefore driven forward, if not by social movements, then at least by class struggles.

It is true that for a very long time racial thinking itself has, in a way, associated class with race. Boulainvilliers, for example, in his *Essai sur la noblesse* (1732), expresses the view that the nobility originates in the 'Frankish race' and the commoners in the 'Gallic race', and the idea that social classes originate in peoples or nations is found in many nineteenth-century historians, such as Augustin Thierry or François Guizot. Closer to our own day, a writer like Abraham Léon developed the argument – though not very convincingly since it runs counter to the facts – that the Jews constitute a 'class people'.[4] But, if we are looking to link racism to class relations, it is better to turn first to a recent, Marxist tradition inaugurated by Oliver Cox's classic work *Caste, Class and Race*, published in 1948 and ignored or rejected by academic sociology at the time.[5] That tradition mainly developed in the 1960s and 1970s, largely in the USA and Britain, where there is still a great deal of life in it.

In his founding work, and subsequently in other writings, Cox broke with the dominant thinking of the 1930s and 1940s in the USA and refused to see race relations in terms of a caste structure, that is, in terms of a mode of relating which excludes conflict and which, in his view, it was quite improper to apply to any other society but India.[6] Drawing on the sociology of caste, particularly the work of Célestin Bouglé,[7] he roundly criticized Dollard and Myrdal, whom he saw as ignoring the class conflict which pitted the American southern oligarchy against the workers, both white and black, and according much too great a role to 'poor whites' in the oppression of the blacks. He also attacked Warner and his description of a 'caste line' running asymmetrically through society and cutting diagonally across class relations, making the whites predominant in the dominant strata and the blacks predominant in the lowest, but not preventing the existence of a white proletariat or a black bourgeoisie.[8] For Cox, racism is the product of capitalism and is propagated by the dominant class to justify and maintain the exploitation of the workers.

Many writers have subsequently criticized Cox for his crude Marxism and have opened up discussions – and broadened the existing debates – in which the reference to class conflicts has occupied a more or less central position. Some have attempted to situate the problem in a planetary context, linking racism with the globalization of the economy and the generalized expansion of capitalism. Thus, for example, Immanuel Wallerstein, continuing a line of thinking begun by Cox, asserts that, when it comes to maximizing capital accumulation and minimizing the costs entailed (political disturbances, demands from the labour force), racism provides 'the magic formula that reconciles these objectives'.[9] Others have preferred to engage in what are perhaps less ambitious analyses, often backed up by empirical data limited to a single country – or a single town or region and even a single neighbourhood – and ask generally more precise questions, such as: Do the socially dominated groups characterized by race form a lower stratum of the working class or an entirely separate entity which detaches from it to form an 'underclass' distinct from the white workers? Are they a class fraction or a reserve army of capital? Does racism function as an ideology independent of class relations but enabling those relations to be reproduced? Is it not, rather, the product of those relations? And so on. These discussions, in which researchers as important as John Rex and Robert Miles have taken part, cannot be reduced to the mere pairing of 'race and class', but they represent a relatively distinct set of preoccupations, a family of debates.[10]

The tradition Cox inaugurated focusses on racism against black people. It is not the only one to have taken up the question of the relation between race and class: from the publication in 1843 of the young Marx's essay on the Jewish question to the rise of Nazism in Germany, Marxism has also furnished a second perspective which has been mainly concerned with the part played by particular classes in anti-semitism and its onward march towards the final solution. A wealth of historical writing on Nazism, subtly and intelligently surveyed by Pierre Ayçoberry,[11] offers all kinds of arguments concerning big capital, the working class and, more especially, the middle classes, and attempts have even been made – notably in the work of Nicos Poulantzas – to integrate the whole range of these social groups into the analysis.[12] Moreover, a useful discussion of the Marxist debate on the Jewish question is to be found in the work of Enzo Traverso, his conclusion being that the history of this debate is the 'history of a failure of understanding'.[13]

With regard to racism against blacks and against Jews, then, there is a quite immense corpus of interpretations connecting two problems – the division of society into classes and the existence of racism. But these approaches can only be of very little assistance to us in respect of the questions we wish to raise. Our concern is not to examine whether capitalism produces racism, either directly or indirectly; nor is it to establish whether the working class is an homogeneous or heterogeneous set of fractions, some of which, as a consequence of racism, might be relegated to the lowest reaches of society or marginalized to become an element of the underclass; nor is it to distribute the various social groups as a function of their relation to racism or to see how racism may possibly function as an ideology permitting, via the state, the reproduction of a social structure while at the same time distorting it where necessary. Our aim, rather, is to study the connections between two patterns of social action, two types of behaviour: on the one hand, behaviour which falls within the ambit of a social movement, in the precise sense of this term within the sociology of action, and, on the other, behaviour which comes under the heading of racism.

This approach has several advantages over one cast in terms of 'race and class'. It allows us, first of all, rather than reducing class to race or attempting to articulate the two, to focus on the conditions which, so far as social movements are concerned, encourage or discourage the expression of racism – either within those social movements or in the wider society; in other words, it leads us to look at the production of racism on the basis of the condition [l'état] of social actors. Secondly, our approach allows us to avoid the dead-ends which the 'race and class' problematic repeatedly runs into. If that approach is not to engage in the absolute reduction of race to class, then, as has been observed by two such different commentators as Étienne Balibar and Floya Anthias, it almost always has to bring in additional external categories such as nation or ethnic group. Balibar observes that the question of the class basis of racism is 'misconceived' and calls for it to be replaced by that of 'the relations between racism, as a supplement to nationalism, and the irreducibility of class conflict in society'; he also calls for an examination of 'how the development of racism displaces class conflict' and transforms it.[14] After a detailed examination of the literature on 'race and class', Anthias finds that the nation and ethnicity are 'central organizing principles of social relations in the modern age'.[15]

We shall go on to deal, at some length, with the relations between nation and race, or rather between communal movements (including nationalist movements) and racism. For the moment, however, it seems possible to assert that our perspective allows us – much more than would a 'race and class' approach – to single out specific problems and deal with the connection between racism and society without our thinking on these matters being interfered with, destroyed or weakened by the introduction of elements analytically external to the debate. To remove any possible misunderstanding, let us add that it is our aim here, for the moment, to confront an important, but particular dimension of racism, not to offer a general theory of the phenomenon, since this would be to leave out of account, among other dimensions, the role of the dominant actors, which we clearly have no intention of denying or minimizing.

2. The destructuring of social movements

There are always two aspects to a social movement. On the one hand, its action is, in effect, counter-offensive, being based on its capacity to develop a project: it puts forward a positive principle – a competence, knowledge or skill. From another angle, however, the actor is mainly on the defensive, and speaks in the name of those with fewest resources, who are defined by deprivation, exclusion and exploitation and have no positive principle to advance. The experience of the labour movement is paradigmatic here.[16]

Some workers can draw on a base of skills to build up struggles in which the highest of their demands poses a challenge to the continued control of industrial production and progress by employers regarded as parasitic or superfluous; the unskilled workers, by contrast, take action against poverty, low wages, the precariousness of the labour market, and join in struggles in which they possess far fewer resources than the craft or skilled workers. The labour movement is never so powerful or integrated or capable of addressing the level where the most general orientations of social life are decided as when it manages to bind together the proud consciousness of the craft workers threatened with de-skilling and the proletarian consciousness of the labourers, the semi-skilled and, more broadly, those workers devoid of any skills whatever.[17]

Throughout the history of the labour movement, this need for integration has always run up against a great many obstacles – the employers' ability to divide the workers, resistance on the part of the more skilled workers to allying with pure proletarians, political and ideological divergences between workers' organizations, etc. Among these obstacles, racism, whenever it is present, always constitutes a major source – or is an expression – of the weakness or destructuring of the actor.

And yet we have to be more precise and recognize here, in the rise of racism against the background of a decomposing social movement, not one single logic at work, but two.

The first of these directly expresses the actor's lack of structuring [*non-structuration*] and incapacity to integrate into a single struggle elements which are dissociated and opposed in racial terms; the second, more complex logic expresses a loss of meaning which will vent itself in hatred of a scapegoat who is totally external to the actor, who barely belongs to the actor's system of action at all, and is in no way an element fragmented off from that system. We shall draw on the experience of American trade unionism to illustrate the first of these two logics and that of the Solidarity union in Poland for the second.

1. The formation of American trade unionism

Very early in the history of the American labour movement, the question arose whether black workers were to be admitted into the unions. Putting aside moral and humanistic considerations and arguments stressing the advantages to be gained in certain very precise situations from non-segregation, the issue of the integration of black workers has often been seen in terms of the construction of a social movement.

Here, for example, are the words of Robert Baker, speaking in 1902 to the Central Labor Union of Brooklyn:

> The more organized labor champions the cause of all labor, unorganized as well as organized, black as well as white, the greater will be the victories; the more lasting, the more permanent, the more beneficial and the more far-reaching will be its successes. If it would extend and broaden its influence . . . it must persistently and vigorously attack special privilege in every form; it must make the cause of humanity, regardless of race, color or sex, its cause.[18]

However, though it was possible, even from the earliest days of American trade unionism, to present the issue – and wish it to be resolved – in this way, in practice that unionism was for many years built on very different foundations.

Until 1935 in fact, segregation greatly predominated over integration among organized labour in the USA. At the time of its foundation in 1881, the movement based on the white 'craft unions' which together formed the American Federation of Labour (AFL) spoke hazily of anti-discriminatory principles, and appealed to morality and reason (wasn't it better to have the negroes with you than against you in a strike?). But this initially firm rejection of a 'colour line' very soon wavered and the humanist rhetoric of the main leader of the AFL, Samuel Gompers, gave way to an increasingly racist policy, even on the part of Gompers himself, who slid steadily into an increasing emphasis on black people's responsibility for the attitudes of the unions.

If the trade unions recruited few black members, the argument ran, wasn't this because the blacks were traitors to the working class, because they broke strikes, accepted poverty wages, weren't prepared to partici-pate in urban life and even less in trade union action; wasn't it ultimately the case that they excluded themselves? This was perverse reasoning and, in his famous analysis of the mechanism of self-fulfilling prophecy, Robert Merton has shown how it reversed the order of the facts and created what it condemned: it was, in fact, because they were refused entry to the big trade unions – and this was massively the case before 1935 – that American blacks became strike-breakers or lowered the price of labour, having no alternative if they were to survive.[19] In reality, for more than half a century American trade unionism refused to link up with the proletarian black and unskilled masses and the few attempts to go against that orientation were always very short-lived.

The Knights of Labor, set up in 1869 with the aim of unifying whites and blacks (but refusing, when the question arose, to accept Chinese workers as members), grew like wildfire (from 20,151 members in 1879 to almost a million at their peak in 1886), but declined no less rapidly – a fact which cannot be explained merely by the violence of the repression they suffered. By 1893 they had no more than 200,000 members and there were great divergences between the whites, who tended to be skilled, and the unskilled blacks. Blacks left the organization in droves, while its leaders called on the federal government to find the necessary funds to deport the blacks to Africa; by 1895, there were only 20,000 members and the experience was historically at an end.

The Industrial Workers of the World (IWW), founded in 1905, were to attempt something much more impressive. They advocated an industrial unionism, which meant that skilled men, the semi-skilled and labourers could all be members of the same union and workers could be defended without regard to skill, colour, sex or national origin. In spite of their intransigent rejection of all discrimination, their spectacular rise produced only modest levels of recruitment among black workers and they collapsed at the end of the First World War, falling victim to very intense repression (their leaders and activists were arrested and given very heavy sentences for 'seditious' activities in time of war) and, even more importantly, to internal ideological dissensions concerning the attitude to be adopted towards the fledgling Soviet Union and the demands of the Communist International.

If no large-scale attempt to build a trade unionism open to all met with success in the United States before 1935, the efforts of blacks to create their own unions did not achieve anything significant either, the chief exception being the Brotherhood of Sleeping Car Porters. This was set up in 1925 by a socialist activist, A. Philip Randolph, who in 1929 even persuaded the AFL to accept this black-led union into its ranks. We have then, in reality, to wait until 1935 and the very pro-trade union Wagner Act and the establishment of the Congress of Industrial Organizations (CIO) for the labour movement to make a clear commitment to organize all workers without discrimination and to open its doors on a stable basis to black workers, who are today disproportionately represented in the trade union movement.[20]

Up to that point, American trade unionism was dominated by white workers, who were most often skilled and able at least to influence pay rates and the labour market, but who engaged in segregation on a massive scale to keep out a large proportion of the working population. They even contributed at times to the unleashing of racial violence, as was notably the case in East St Louis (Illinois) in July 1917, when, in a tense situation, the AFL spread rumours that 15,000 blacks were about to arrive, allegedly called in by the local employers, and thus contributed to (and perhaps even organized) the riots which killed some forty members of the black population. Rejected by the dominant trade unionism and powerless to acquire structures of their own, or only admitted into fragile unions which soon broke up and which, as they fell apart, were likely (as we have seen with the Knights of Labor) to give rise to a racism that negated the spirit in which they were originally founded, the black proletariat found itself either excluded from action or, at times, the victim of the action of others.

The American labour movement was built up in a period when large black populations were coming together in the great industrial cities. There they encountered what was at times a heightened degree of racism, but they could also find jobs and participate in modern urban life. In many historical experiences, a social movement has formed as a result of the integration of the proud consciousness of the craft workers and the proletarian consciousness of the labourers and their like. In this case, the formation of such a movement was restricted as a result of racism, which contributed to a remoteness towards – and a rejection of – blacks by the whites, who were in general more skilled and better placed in the job market.

Clearly, the history of racism and that of the labour movement in the United States are not one and the same, and the transformations occurring within each of these histories only affect the other in very partial ways. But the American labour movement experience is certainly that of an essentially white social actor, which proved unable, in its formative phase, to take up the cause of the proletariat as a whole and which often preferred racism to real attempts to bring the totality of the workers together in a single struggle.

2. The decline of Solidarity

As we have just seen, in the phase in which a social movement is forming, racism puts a brake on the development of an action which is able to represent all the workers and speak up for a more just and humane society. By the same token, the crisis or decline of a social movement may possibly open up a space for the rise of racist discourse or behaviour. The experience of Solidarity in Poland gives a concrete illustration of this phenomenon.[21] It also provides an example of processes in which racism becomes directed not against an element which could play a part in the formation of a social movement, but against a scapegoat almost wholly external to it, and, moreover, absent, or virtually absent, from the general political and social scene.

At its origin in August 1980, Solidarity seemed to be the product of the remarkable historical convergence of three distinct struggles. It was a total social movement: a simultaneous expression of workers' trade union action, national assertiveness and a political battle for democratic rights and freedoms.[22] At the point where they converged, these three constituent elements left no room for any kind of anti-semitism. There were, admittedly, no more than a few thousand Jews in Poland, a country which had been home to some three million before the war; but this in itself means nothing, since there had been frequent outbreaks of a Jew-less anti-semitism before 1980 and, as we shall see, others were to follow later.

In fact, in 1980, everything seemed to militate against the new trade union showing the slightest inclination to anti-semitism. The Polish workers had long since succumbed to massification; they had no capacity for action and were generally steeped in a popular culture hostile to the Jews, the people who had allegedly killed Christ and whom many blamed for having helped to bring communism to power and for managing it. But their adversary was not a mythic Jew – real Jews having in fact been expelled from all sites of power since the 'purges' which came to a head in 1968 – but a clearly identified enemy: the party in power.

The movement's democratic project, which owed much to the intellectuals' commitment to the struggle, also had nothing whatever to do with racial hatred. Lastly, the national component, which was indissociable from a powerful and very influential Catholicism, seemed far removed from the anti-semitism which had generally accompanied both religious and nationalist discourse in Poland. Since Vatican II, and even more clearly since the election of Cardinal Wojtyla as pope, the Polish church had put its anti-Jewish sentiments behind it and increasingly distanced itself from any anti-semitic themes. In fact, if these were present in the Poland of 1980, they were to be found mainly in certain government circles, or close to them, and in some very marginal Catholic groupings, where they had no influence on the emerging social movement.

And yet, a year later, the picture had changed. The first signs of a new climate could be detected at the Solidarity congress of September 1981. These became clearer in the following months, particularly with the Jurczyk affair, which takes its name from an important leader of the movement, an historic figure in the workers' struggles of 1970 at Szczecin, who called publicly in the November for the communist leaders and the Jews governing the country to be hanged.

Behind this episode, what was really occurring was that the structure of the movement was beginning to collapse. This was to become clearer in the period of clandestinity and clearer yet at the dawn of the new era in Poland in 1989 when the trade unions were legalized again and the country was able to assert its political independence. The period after autumn 1981 saw the development of a process of dissociation, under the influence of the economic crisis and the political impasse, in which the disintegrative tendencies lying within the most defensive aspect of the new social actor found expression. The negotiation-based trade unionism of Lech Wałesa was denounced by those – and there were more and more of them – exasperated by food shortages or by the increasing impossibility of maintaining production in the factories; the nationalists hardened their line and appealed increasingly to community, Polishness and homogeneity, as well as calling from time to time for a return to order and firm government. Uncompromising workerism and nationalism joined together to form a sinister populism, ominously charged with a critique increasingly hostile to the intellectuals and political leaders of the movement most closely associated with its democratic agenda: and in this destructuring, which provides evidence, already, that the actor really had been weakened, a space opened up for a diffuse anti-semitism appropriate both to an exasperated, radicalized grassroots – the movement's dark side – and to hypernationalist ideologues – 'true Poles', who continued to gain steadily in importance throughout the 1980s. These latter were populists re-discovering the path of a conservative Catholicism symbolized by the Primate of Poland, Cardinal Glemp, who was to make world headlines in 1989 with his anti-semitic declarations regarding the Carmelite nunnery at Auschwitz.

Ten years after the formation of a total social movement a watershed had indeed been reached in Poland and the Jewish question was once more a spectre haunting the country, which had now entered the post-Solidarity era. More than ever, anti-semitism was directed against a mythic enemy: the few Jews who held any kind of responsible positions in political, intellectual or trade union life (often targeted, even though there were only a handful of them) and the cosmopolitan Jews to be found all over the Western world, who were said to hold the levers of command, money, political power and the media. During the rise of the Solidarity movement, any temptation to engage in anti-semitism had been kept at bay; the decline of that movement, however relative, produced the opposite: the diffuse, but easily observable upsurge of an anti-semitism which occupied the space left vacant by the social movement.

The experiences we have just examined are exemplary on two distinct counts. First of all, both illustrate our hypothesis that there is a link between social movements and racism. The anti-black racism of the white American workers occurred in the early stages, in the period of formation of the social movement; the anti-semitism came in the later stages, in the period when Solidarity was growing weaker. But in both cases, we are dealing with the same phenomenon. These two historical experiences also indicate that the destructuring of a social movement may be associated with two types of racism which differ fundamentally from each other. In the one, the victim group is involved in the action, or could be, and aspires to be; in the other, the hatred expressed is directed at a group which is essentially alien to the social actor concerned and even has no great concrete existence on the relevant internal scene. Lastly, in the former experience a logic of inferiorization is dominant, but it is associated also with a logic of differentiation and exclusion, whereas in the latter, only a logic of a differentialist type is present.

10

TWO PATTERNS OF RACISM

Insofar as it arises out of the weakness or breakdown of a social movement, racism is not merely a consequence of that process, totally divorced from the movement in its content. The significations it expresses maintain a connection with the meaning which is being lost; they are not wholly dissociated from the relations of which the social movement is itself one of the terms. But they denature that connection, invent new, mythical relations, distort or invert the meaning which provides the social move-ment with its reference points: thus, in their opposition to the blacks, the white American trade unionists spoke of the betrayal of the working class; the anti-semitism which welled up within Solidarity was directed against the ascendancy or domination of the Jews, presented as the cause of the movement's setbacks and failures, as enemies of the cause. The themes on which racism plays move away from the themes of the social movement, but these latter are not so much forgotten as disfigured. This is why racism can be conceived as a negation of the social movement, and why we are led, as a result, to the notion of a social anti-movement.

1. The notion of social anti-movement

A social anti-movement is not exactly the reverse image of a social movement. It is made up of the same key elements, but these are considerably shunted around and transformed and the anti-movement is incapable of integrating them into action – a fact which finds expression in either the dissociation or fusional totalization of these elements.

This notion, which we take from the work of Alain Touraine,[1] is an analytic construct which takes account, on the one hand, of the three principles constitutive of social actors, and, on the other, of the modes in which these principles are combined.

(a) In the social anti-movement the social identity of the actor is replaced by a reference to a being, an essence, a nature, by an identification with a cultural, moral or religious category – the forces of good, or justice – or, alternatively, with a mythical social figure, such as the working class, when this latter either does not exist or does not in any way recognize itself in the discourse of the actor. In the case of racism, the actor does not act in the name of the workers, of parents or any other specific social category; that actor speaks on behalf of a race which itself regards the other races as inferior or as not belonging to humanity;

(b) In the social anti-movement the image of a social adversary, which constitutes the principle of opposition in a social movement, dissolves and gives way to a double representation. Here, in effect, the actor may be ranged either against an enemy with whom it is implacably at war, or against an abstract, relatively indeterminate system which is more or less mythical in nature. The Other is no longer a real actor; he is either naturalized and objectivized or identified with a meta-social principle – for example: evil, the devil or decadence. Apart from the fact that he is supposed to be hatching plots, secretly manipulating power, undermining the actor in malevolent and mysterious ways, he becomes extremely distant and elusive, or, by contrast, may seem very close and concrete, but in this latter case he is reduced to a non-human or infra-human category – which enables him to be kept at a distance or identified with animality or makes it permissible for lethal violence to be used against him. It is in this way that racism arrives at the idea that the Other constitutes a threat, that he is evil and that a ruthless battle has to be waged against him.

(c) Lastly, with the social anti-movement, there is no longer conflict around stakes common to both the social actor and its adversary; there is no longer a shared conception of historicity, recourse to the same language as the adversary in doing battle with him, or a consciousness of acting to control or direct the same set of resources. There is no longer, for example, the idea, shared by the labour movement and the employers, that progress and industry go together and that the point is to manage them, each party acting towards that end. The actor retreats to its own ground and takes the view that there is no positive historicity outside its own; it defines itself by rupture, distance and the retreat into its own conceptions, not by belonging to the same field as its opponents. It becomes sectarian or warlike; it denies the idea of a structural conflict or a social relation; it constitutes a force for historical change or closes itself off from all communication with the outside; its plans are not targeted at the society in which it lives, but directed towards creating an homogeneous, purified unity. From this point of view, racism calls, with varying degrees of emphasis, for the setting apart or elimination of those who are not part of a historicity defined in terms of racial properties – properties which are themselves perceived as indissociable from a culture and a history.

It is the specific property of a social anti-movement that it is incapable of articulating the three principles we have just presented or of integrating them into a single action: it cannot speak in the name of a particular social category and a general, liberatory conception of society; it ceases to recognize stakes that are common to an adversary and to itself; and it quite simply cannot accept internal tensions and debates. As we shall see with regard to racism, it either withdraws into partial and perverted figurations of a social movement, or constitutes itself as a totalizing entity which constructs a system of imaginary action – an unreal and potentially lethal substitute for lost, rejected or impossible social relations.

2. Partial racism, total racism

Between the complete breakdown of a social movement, or even a deep crisis of that movement, and the high point of its development, there are intermediate situations which favour the development of a racism which represents the dark side of that movement and may be described, in more precise terms, as a partial anti-movement.

This scenario involves the coexistence of two logics which give expression to the break-up of the system of action. On the one hand, the actor remains, in effect, engaged in social relations in a conflict which pits it against a clearly defined adversary; on the other hand, it is mobilized in racist practices and discourses which suggest a situation of competition rather than of conflict. This coexistence of two logics may last for as long as the social movement continues to enjoy a certain capacity for action, without, however, attaining a high level of projective content and integration. The effect is that the two logics are mutually limiting. This coexistence of two logics can be seen all the more clearly if we examine the principle structuring the actor's identity.

If the actor is incapable of acting – or powerless to act – in the name of all who are suffering comparable or complementary forms of domination, and if it decides only to defend and promote particular interests, then that means recognizing or introducing a split within the ranks of the population it is seeking to represent. It does, admittedly, continue to call for action and make social demands, but its struggle stops, on non-social criteria, at the point where that struggle might possibly relate to the racialized fraction of the group to which it belongs. It then singles out on racial lines people who can hardly be distinguished from the actor socially by their position within the prevailing relations of domination or, at least, people whom the actor should or could bring together in a single struggle; and it not only ignores these people, but rejects them and fights them.

The identity of the actor is here fragmented and transformed. It breaks up, on the one hand, into sub-identities covering a whole range of particular interests which, though still social, are not universal or general in their scope, and, on the other, into a definition which can no longer be social and becomes racial and racist. This explains how, in the labour movement in particular, racism can arise at the point of conjunction between sectional or corporatist demands and an effort to exclude certain racialized groups – blacks, for example – from the system in which these demands can be formulated.

More broadly, we can say of the partial anti-movement that it emerges in a process of duplication in which, on the one hand, the actor maintains, in a weakened form, an image of an identity and of a social adversary and a consciousness of involvement in a relation of domination, and, on the other hand, engages, in the name of race, in competitive practices on *markets* – particularly the housing and labour markets – where individual strategies and collective pressures, which may possibly be violent and are susceptible of translation to the political level, stand in for action. Whilst it combines these two characteristics, the racism involved here is more inegalitarian than differentialist, especially if those promoting it are able to maintain a social, economic or organizational superiority – for example, by retaining a monopoly on skilled labour and leaving the monotonous, dirty or unpleasant work to the racialized group. It does not necessarily involve an intermediate reference to a community – of nationality or religion, for example, which the Other may very well share. Such racism gives expression to a partial destructuring of the actor, and a state of duplication which permits many a conjunctural oscillation – between movement and anti-movement, social conflict and racial hatred or rejection.

But when the social movement goes into unstoppable decline or undergoes such a crisis that it loses all meaning for some of its protagonists, this phenomenon of duplication gives way to the social void. Here the actor is, as it were, cut free of all moorings in a social relationship; it is not – or not any longer – able to find the behavioural markers by which it was previously able to orient its action. It is no longer in a half-way house, as in the case just discussed where it was torn between two systems of action, simultaneously involved in a social conflict and a market; it is no longer located within a conflictual social field, or this no longer has any meaning for it. And, among the various possibilities – apathy or consumerist individualism, for example – there opens up the scenario of the formation of a racism which reconstructs, in imaginary mode, a fictive system of action which substitutes itself for the faltering social system. This impressive construction first of all entails the redefinition of the adversary, who now becomes an enemy identified with evil; and it involves the actor not, now, in a conflict, but in discourses of separation and rupture, if not indeed of violence, and is based on a reformulation of the actor's identity which can no longer be fragmented or duplicated, as in the previous case, but which, divested of all social reference, takes on a distinctly communal coloration, even before – or at the same time as – it assumes a racial one. The racism, here, is unlimited. It does not place the actor on a market or in competitive relations with those who share the actor's social condition or are not far removed from it; it takes itself out of this type of reality to establish a new space, dominated by the hate-filled pursuit of a scapegoat. This racism is much more differentialist than inegalitarian. In this sense, too, it is total, as indeed is the anti-movement from which it issues, whereas in the previous case it was merely partial.

3. Racism, social movements and social structure

The reader should not conclude from the preceding discussion that the only source of the growth of racism lies in the destructuring of social movements. This phenomenon, though not exceptional, is not – by a long way – directly responsible for the principal manifestations of racism, and it is not the sad or impotent figures of a movement which has become a social anti-movement that make up the big battalions of racist thinking or action. We must, none the less, continue to explore the idea of a connection between social movements, anti-movements and racism.

When it is powerful and has a high projective content – as was the case with the labour movement in Western societies up to the 1960s – a social movement does not merely have a considerable capacity to mobilize those who, because they have intense experience of the domination it has arisen to combat, immediately recognize themselves in it. Apart from the actions of its most immediate protagonists, it also structures – and confers meaning on – a wide range of behaviours extending far beyond its strict field of action. Thus, in all the places where it was a central reality, the labour movement constituted a reference point for all kinds of actors mobilized in neighbourhood politics, in universities, in cultural or sporting movements, or in action in the name of women, consumers or user-groups, of reformist or revolutionary political projects and also of grand principles such as justice and democracy, without those actors (and the above list is not an exhaustive one) necessarily having to regard themselves as sharing in a working-class social identity. And when such a central figure declines, when the reference point it represented becomes increasingly artificial or ideological, the actors to whom it offered a meaningful place are orphaned and weakened; they lose their capacity to see their specific practice as part of a more general struggle and also lose a political lever which enabled them to feel part of the relation structuring the whole of social life.

Hence the weakness, breakdown or absence of social movements exerts substantial, though indirect, effects on racism, particularly in a working-class milieu.

1. Racism and social exclusion

A first illustration of this phenomenon concerns the world of social outcasts and is provided by the experience, already mentioned in Chapter 7, of the 'underclass' formed by the blacks in the American 'hyperghettos'. These people are not in a position to mobilize the resources required for collective action; even action of a 'Black-Power' type, with a potentially high exemplary or violent content, seems precluded in their case.

When, responding to the attraction of the urban, industrial world, American blacks moved up from the South, particularly after 1910 or 1915, they could see themselves as a proletariat, as part of the working class – even when the white labour unions rejected them. They could exert social pressure, gain a hearing from some trade unionists, appeal to the idea of a labour movement and insist their plight not be dissociated from that of the other workers. Even if they were poverty-stricken, they were not marginalized and could give a social meaning to their demands. Those who live in the hyperghetto today belong to a world which has become detached from the rest of society, including, as Wilson points out, from the black lower-middle class.[2] They can, if they so wish, kill one another, destroy themselves either with drugs or in a world of petty crime largely bounded by their own social space, and sink into poverty; they have hardly anything like the symbolic – or the political, organized – way-stations which the labour movement brought them, however inadequate these may have been, nor do they have even the aspiration to participate in such a movement. The breakdown of that movement, which certainly reached its peak somewhere between the 1930s and the 1950s or 1960s, makes the combination of racism and socio-economic exclusion more acute than ever. It enables the white working classes to get by better, as a result of the tremendous dualization which now separates them from the poverty-stricken black masses, who are pushed aside and left to their own devices – at best, to social welfare – and for whom social exclusion and economic difficulties are now so much of a concern that, paradoxically, racism has become a secondary issue. To put it another way, as long as a labour movement existed, the conditions for the expansion of anti-black racism were limited by a project of collective action in which all workers were united without distinction of race. From the point where this began to break up, millions of blacks – and not only blacks – found themselves defined by poverty, under-employment and unemployment and by their confinement in the vast expanses of the hyperghetto, where they are totally segregated and excluded and, as the victims of industrial and urban change in which an undeniably racist sorting process has taken place, take no part in the country's social debates and conflicts. For some decades, the social movement was able to keep alive the hope – and also, to some extent, the reality – of a socio-economic integration that was stronger than racism; with the historic decline of that movement, the project of social integration has given way, for many, to a total – racial and social – segregation.

2. The drift within the middle classes

A second illustration of the phenomenon we are concerned with here relates to the middle classes in the broad sense; contemporary French experience provides us with a particularly significant example.

As is the case throughout the Western world, the middle classes in France form a vast and thoroughly heterogeneous ensemble and exert considerable political and cultural influence. Up until the 1970s, when political and social life was organized around the central conflict which ranged the labour movement against the employers, the middle classes were, so to speak, polarized, having no option but to take up positions by reference to the two social adversaries who, through their struggle, gave society its structure. A copious literature, generally Marxist in inspiration, sought at the time to account for this phenomenon of polarization.[3] There is nothing to suggest that the middle classes were, at that stage, fundamentally any more or less racist than they are today. But the debates which they took a hand in constructing were dominated by a sense that society was structured by a central divide and their commitments were largely determined by that divide. These classes, which were politically and culturally active, participated in the public action Albert Hirschman writes of,[4] and the presence of immigrants was certainly not a question which concerned them obsessively – immigration, though already a mass phenomenon, being defined at that time in terms not of population, but of labour.

The crisis of industrial society and, most especially, the decline of the labour movement have also demobilized these classes, to the point that many writers, their attention fixed on this vast range of social categories – and on them alone – have felt able to speak of a social void, of narcissism and a generalized individualism. Within a few years, in fact, the middle classes have seemed to lose all interest in any wide-ranging collective commitment and to go over solely to the pursuit of private happiness. The breakdown of the conflict which structured society propelled them, as it were, into a new universe, where their problem could no longer be one of situating themselves with regard to this general principle of organization but of finding their place on the ladder of social stratification. Being as far away from power as they are from the world of the social outcasts, they seem to belong to a society which is, for the moment, defined more by participation in consumption, by mobility, and by opportunities for going up in the world and the danger of going down. The transition from a class society to a society of stratification and exclusion, and also the waning of the new social movements – in which they played a considerable part in the 1970s – have found expression, where they are concerned, in many kinds of effects which are all, more or less, linked to their relative position on the social ladder. And, among these effects, the one which concerns us most is the opening up of a wider space for attitudes and behaviours which tend towards racism or border upon it. On the one hand, the middle classes – and even the least deprived of the lower classes – have attempted to mark themselves off not so much from the poor or the manual workers [*le monde ouvrier*] as from the immigrant population, which has increasingly come to be perceived as an ethnic and religious threat. They have deserted certain areas and moved to homogeneous suburbs; they have resorted to private education or to special dispensations, often based on personal favours, to take their children out of schools with a high level of immigrants, thus creating the beginnings of a social and ethnic segregation which is itself imbued with a certain racism. And, on the other hand, in the political crisis opened up by the decline of industrial society and the political forces which were its representatives, they have contributed indirectly to the rise of a populism which has found its chief expression in the Front national, a party in which racism, including anti-semitism, has its place.

Those sustaining this populism are not necessarily the same people who have managed to develop the individual strategies which are leading to a *de facto* segregation. Indeed, it is found much more among those who do not have the resources to permit them to adopt such strategies – who see their neighbourhood deteriorating, for example, or who end up in a run-down urban environment; it is the expression of an incapacity to offset the loss of the reference points once provided by classic industrial society in any other way than by reconstituting new ones on a xenophobic and racializing basis.[5]

Here again, there is not one single logic at work, but two. The first of these – a segregative logic – keeps a racialized population at bay, avoids living in the same places as they do and marks its distance from people who signify both social decline and a different racial identity. The second builds up the racialized group – primarily, in the French case, the populations originating from the Maghreb – into a threat and a scapegoat. There is a constant interplay between these two logics and they are difficult to disentangle in practice. But they are distinct, and the way they differ is of the same order as the way partial racism differs from total.

4. The two modes of the social production of racism

The notions of social movement and anti-movement thus allow us to elucidate the possible expansion of racism in a way which goes far beyond the actors most directly concerned. They also allow us to bring out clearly two fundamentally different modes of the social production of racism which we had already begun to identify when we were examining the theme of prejudice (Chapter 6) or the concrete experiences of American or Polish trade unionism (Chapter 9).

On the one hand, racism appears as a perversion of social relations, a degraded form of social behaviour, the space for which grows larger when the society in question is not highly structured by the existence of a social movement. For racism to appear, certain conditions must be fulfilled in both the racializing and the racialized groups. The racializing group must possess resources which remain social and a capacity for – individual or collective – action which is linked to economic or political means, to a status – even a threatened one – or, alternatively, to degrees of freedom in the recourse to violence or to a certain tolerance or permissiveness within the political system and the institutions. Racist behaviours find a favourable terrain in the existence of markets in which these resources are often sufficient to ensure discrimination, to force an inferior status on the Other in the spheres of job-seeking or employment or, alternatively, to bring about urban or educational segregation.

Such behaviours are also encouraged by the victim group bearing certain characteristics which are, to use John Dollard's terms, 'visible' – that is, the existence of physical or cultural markers which make any individual who belongs to the racialized population easily identifiable.[6]

On the other hand, racism appears as the totally imaginary construction of a system of action, the delusional invention of relations between races, the radical shift from a concrete, real stage to a fictive one, to a natural or cosmic order in which it is directed against a scapegoat.

This shift again implies resources, but these are not so much social as symbolic, historical and cultural in character; it involves a definition of the actor in terms of community – most often in terms of nation – by the activation or reactivation of myths rooted in what may be a history of substantial density – as is the case with anti-Jewish racism.

Here again, the choice of scapegoat is not accidental or conjunctural, at least in the case of those experiences which are to some degree stable over time (hatred of Jews and Gypsies in particular). If we follow Gordon W. Allport, we have to say that it owes much to historical and cultural factors specific to the victim group; it is based, as Yves Chevalier writes, with specific reference to the case of anti-semitism, on the fact that the Jews are 'a minority group with an identity of its own, and one that is geographically dispersed and which generally occupies partially – and, indeed, increasingly – distinct economic positions, and which has long maintained not unambiguous relations with the authorities'.[7]

These two modes of the social production of racism bring us back to the opposition we have already established between differentialist and inegalitarian racism, though the two sets of terms do not overlap exactly.[8] They are, however, sufficiently close for us to link partial racism with the predominantly inegalitarian variant, on the one hand, and total racism with the predominantly differentialist form, on the other. In some instances, these occur in succession, as though it were the case, in particular, that the exhaustion or impossibility of partial racism culminated in transition to a total racism. For example, the 'skinheads' first made their appearance as a manifestation of the British labour movement in its decomposition, as a form without social content, disconnected from any class conflict, still bearing the stamp of a certain working-class culture and carrying a charge of anger which soon went beyond partial anti-black or, more commonly anti-Asian racism – so frequently encountered among white workers – to develop, in a space which had extended to Europe, into a total neo-Nazi-inspired racism unconnected with any form of working-class action or with strategies on the labour or housing markets. In other cases, it would be more exact to speak of an intermediate zone, where the attempt to maintain a social order in which partial racism has its place combines with tendencies to move towards a total racism. This is, more or less, the territory of the 'poor white', whether we are speaking of the barbaric violence of popular lynchings in the USA, which went on into the 1920s, or, to take contemporary France, of that infra-racist populism in which the actor oscillates between a desire to keep the immigrants in a state of subordination and inferiority and a hate-filled call for their deportation.

This brings us to one final comment: the two modes of social production of racism just presented, which correspond to analytic categories, should not be confused with historical phenomena. Taken overall, such phenomena may very well involve one or other of these categories to a greater or lesser extent, but they may also involve both, and considerable degrees of variation over time and space may also occur. Though anti-black racism has most often been associated historically with practices of domination and with an inegalitarian or partial logic – as we have just seen with the example of the 'poor whites' – it also comprises a differentialist dimension which is not far removed from a total racism. By the same token, anti-semitism should not be seen as always – or exclusively – obeying the logic of total racism. Thus, in a robustly argued piece, Jacob Katz takes to task three types of explanation – the 'socio-political', the 'psychoanalytic' and the 'ideological' – which have in common a neglect of the real conflicts between Jews and non-Jews.[9] There are, explains Katz, three ways of detaching anti-semitism from its connection with real, concrete Jews: the first consists in seeing it as a displacement of social protests on to a group which provided an easier target than the real culprits; the second, exemplified by Saül Friedländer's book on Nazi anti-semitism, reduces the phenomenon to a collective psychosis;[10] the third puts the emphasis on the strength of racial ideology, leaving out of account the actual existence of Jews. It is true that anti-semitism, fictive as it may seem, generally develops in situations where there is a certain genuine Jewish presence, where Jews form more or less visible communities, and where some of them occupy economic, social, political or cultural positions. It is also true that anti-semitism without Jews is an extreme case and one which is historically exceptional, being met hardly anywhere but in Communist or post-Communist central Europe or, on a much smaller scale, in contemporary Japan.[11] It is certainly true that, in some cases, anti-semitism falls under the heading of what, keeping to our terminology, we must call partial racism, as is very well illustrated by Victor Karady and Istvan Kémény in the case of inter-war Hungary, where the rise of anti-semitism occurred against a backdrop of competition with Jews on the labour and education markets.[12] But in very many cases, one would be missing the essential point if one were not sensitive to the imaginary and symbolic function performed by the Jews and the differentialist logic which rejects all conflict, and even all market competition with them, and calls for them to be set apart and destroyed. In its historical forms, anti-semitism frequently combines the two basic logics of racism; but if it occupies a central place in history, this assuredly has more to do with the expulsions and frenzied massacres which have been associated with it than with the inegalitarian relations it has very often been seen to accompany or used to rationalize.

11

COMMUNAL IDENTITY AND RACISM

It is rare for a racist act or discourse, however isolated it might seem, not to appeal to a reference community in which race is associated in various ways with other identity-related referents.

In the modern world, the nation is the category which inevitably performs this role, even if it is not necessarily linked – in virtually consubstantial fashion – to a (more often differentialist than inegalitarian) racism, which grounds or accompanies the promotion or purification of the nation or its defence against an external threat. But it would seem, at this first approximation, that there are also other types of community which should properly command our attention.

One of these is religion and, in particular, Christianity, which played a considerable role in European colonial expansion and inspired what were often racist practices long before the concept of racism existed. For did it not take the vigorous intervention of Las Casas on their behalf – among other actions – for the American Indians, whom church and state were reluctant to regard as having souls, to be recognized as human beings? And, to stay for a moment in the Spain of the Inquisition at what Léon Poliakov terms its 'fateful hour',[1] was it not the same alliance of church and state which, with the 'purity of blood' laws, invented the first truly political and biological version of what, up until the fifteenth century, had been more an anti-Jewish sentiment with faintly biologizing tendencies than a racism properly so-called? Even in a minute quantity, explains a sixteenth-century controversialist quoted by Charles Amiel, Jewish blood corrupts a man; it is *quasi venenum* (like poison)![2]

Another such category is ethnicity. Since the 1970s many writers have noted a resurgence of this phenomenon, revealing the failure of evolution-ist thinking and of the idea that modernization and industrialization would prove to be irreversible solvents of this kind of particularism. Ethnicity and race are so closely intermingled for many researchers and specialists that the two terms are regularly found together, as for example in the titles of several recent works, the name of an important journal and the title of one of the research committees of the International Sociological Association.[3] And yet the notion of ethnicity is problematic in many ways. It is not always clear how it is to be distinguished from the concept of nationality, even if Max Weber does confer a political character on the nation which he refuses to grant to the 'ethnic group'. One sometimes has the impression, as we have seen, that speaking of ethnicity allows a more or less explicitly racial definition of the group concerned to be re-introduced by the back door, or, alternatively, that the term provides a cover for social problems to which it is unwilling to refer directly.

Given its unstable or fragile character, the term 'ethnicity' very evidently breaks up in the literature into three different types of notion. In the first case, it is quite close to the concept of nationhood, as for example in the work of a writer like Anthony D. Smith who uses the term 'ethnic nationalism' to refer to the doctrine and action of those who, since the end of the eighteenth century, have claimed the status of nation and hence also the right to self-determination and an independent state for every ethnic group.[4] In the second case, the biological aspects take precedence over the social and cultural, a tendency which one finds, surprisingly, in the most recent writings of one of the best analysts of racism, Pierre L. van den Berghe, who is now putting forward a bio-social theory of ethnic populations and, particularly, of racism itself, which he ultimately explains much more in terms of genetics than of any other discipline.[5] In the third and last variant, exemplified by the work of Stephen Steinberg among others, the object is to inquire into the social relations which are concealed, mythically or ideologically, by recourse to the notion of ethnicity.[6]

Nation, religion and ethnic group are not the only communities which can provide reference points for the racist actor. We could add many others, such as the sect, the tribe, the clan and the town or region, for example. But the key point is that, above and beyond the distinctions one can find between the different forms of community, they all seem to provide a favourable terrain for the growth of racism. But we have to be much more precise about what we are arguing here.

1. Community and communal action

Classical sociology speaks a great deal of communities and we might even say that it was very largely built up around the contrasting conceptual pairing of community and society, together with the idea of a general forward march of history leading from the one to the other: from *Gemeinschaft* to *Gesellschaft*, from mechanical to organic solidarity, from ascription to achievement. Community, as Ferdinand Tönnies explains, for example, is an ancient form of life in which social relations are lived and felt rather than abstractly conceived. In communities, no-one is distanced from their practice; one finds ties of family and blood, instinct and pleasure, custom and rite.[7] The analysis here centres on the functioning and organization of the collectivity. It may also take a descriptive turn, seeking objectively to characterize diverse forms of communities with the aid of cultural, biological and territorial or geographical criteria.

But this style of approach soon reveals its limitations; it isolates one or more human groups to which it attributes particular characteristics, and, in extreme cases, an essence, without explaining either the modifications which may affect these characteristics themselves or, more especially, the action conducted in the name of the community concerned. This is why we have to turn to other approaches which are more responsive to the subjectivity of the communal actors, the basic elements of which are to be found in the work of Max Weber. Weber is, admittedly, more interested in the process by which communities are founded and transformed and he resorts quite widely to the notion of *Vergemeinschaftung** (literally: communalization) to account for phenomena of group formation (or dispersal) or to describe the role of upbringing and education.[8] His main problem, as he clearly states with regard to religion, is action within a community and not the action of that community.[9] But his particular interest in 'emotional' communities and the well-known passages on charisma clear the ground for the idea of communal action: the charismatic leader, a figure peculiar to emotional communities, defines a project, inspires a collective action and gives it a meaning. And, with regard to national feeling, Weber suggests – as he also does when referring to the ethnic community – that the unity of emotions and 'passion'† leads to a 'passionate pride' in one's own political power.[10]

Efforts have sometimes been made to contrast two images of communal action. The one is portrayed as rational and stressing the capacity of ethnic, national or other collectivities to respond in a calculated way to social pressures or to mobilize resources – particularly political resources; the other, by contrast, lays emphasis on the basic, instinctive, regressive predispositions of the same collectivities.[11] In fact, in both these cases, this is to miss the essential point, particularly where communal racism is concerned. This sometimes reduces to a basic hard core which plays a part, at times, in calculations and strategies, but its production is governed much more by processes charged with a freight of meaning. To the extent that it refers to an identity which is other than social, racism has to be envisaged as a particular modality of action, a mobilizing force which belongs to – or is at least associated with – the much wider family of communal movements.

2. The notion of communal movement

A communal movement bears no relation to a social movement since, whereas the latter gives expression to a society's division, a communal movement appeals, by contrast, to the unity of the social body or of any other collectivity. We can, however, give a rudimentary definition of the

---

* *Translator's note*: I have introduced the reference to Weber's original term, '*Vergemein-schaftung*', since this is not uniformly rendered by any single English word or phrase in the published translations.

† *Translator's note*: I have followed Wieviorka in translating Weber's German term '*pathos*' here as 'passion'.

notion by specifying, as with the notion of social movement, the nature of its component elements and the way in which these fit together.

1. Communal identity

The communal movement, which speaks in the name of a particular entity – be it nation, religion, race, ethnic group or whatever – is necessarily built upon an identity. This is the basis of all communal action, no matter what may subsequently be its way of defining what it is opposed to or mobilizing against. The peculiar feature of identity here is that it has need of nothing but itself for its definition, that it implies no relationship between the actor and another actor. That identity constitutes its being, its essence, its nature; it establishes a unity which apparently owes nothing to social relations and which seems, at a first approximation, to constitute an ahistorical or transhistorical given. Communal identity rests on a language, a culture, a religion, etc.; it runs through time, from the past to the present, inclining rather to the one or the other, either towards an original source, a founding moment, or towards a destiny in which there is no reference to a social definition of the actor. That actor is borne along by values or an historical project and is either much more than a social force in conflict with other social forces – humanity, or the bearer of truth, justice or civilization – or is much less – a nature, a being, an essence. It is, at times, a combination of these two principles – both infra– and supra-social.

Whatever the cement of identity – history, culture, religion, etc. – it subordinates the individual (or sub-groups) to a unity of which he is merely one atom and precludes individualism (in the sense intended by Louis Dumont when he contrasts individualism with holism). More precisely, it authorizes the individual to constitute himself as an actor, while preventing him from constituting himself as a subject. The individual, as the smallest element in a unity brought together by traditions or affects, can participate in a collective struggle, be it an offensive or defensive one; he cannot produce his existence by himself, he is not defined by his creative ability or his capacity to make choices by which he might construct his own life. Determination of the meaning of his behaviour is in the hands of those who have the power to inspire or orient action – scholars, prophets, charismatic leaders.

Lastly, to the extent that it appeals to the unity – if not, indeed, homogeneity – of the collectivity, communal identity may go hand in hand with a concern to expel the elements of impurity from that collectivity, to purge it of those elements. This brings us very directly to the theme of differentialist racism.

2. Opposition

A communal movement is defined, secondly, by what or who it regards as its opposition. It may be that a community which is in crisis or externally threatened chooses flight, desertion or self-destruction – as was the case with the Tupi-Guarani, who, as Pierre Clastres explains, opted for 'collective near suicide',[12] or the members of the Peoples' Temple sect who, in 1976, allowed themselves to be massacred by their leaders in Guyana. Neither sectarian closure nor messianism, for example, necessarily implies an engagement in action directed against an enemy, and we have to accept that, precisely because it is not a social movement involved in a conflictual relationship organized around stakes which are common to itself and its adversary, a communal movement may choose between two definitions of its relation to the threat or the enemy and two modes of managing that relation.

Opposition may, in effect, lead to the recognition of an enemy to be combated or negotiated with, but one that is, certainly, to be confronted and, at any event, referred to as an enemy. It may, by contrast, express itself in a rejection of – or inability to achieve – such a recognition. In that case, it may then take on various forms: sectarian withdrawal; a centring upon exemplary behaviour, which closes the group off from the world; or, as mentioned above, flight, self-destruction and dispersal. There is without any doubt a very great diversity both of possible confrontational, war-like and violent behaviours and of behaviours in which opposition is not expressed in the form of face-to-face confrontation with another actor, but denied or rejected and, above all, interiorized or internalized. The point here is that, in the case of communal movements, rather than a simple principle of opposition, which fits closely with the experience of social movements, we have a dual principle, a combination of externalization and internalization which the actor may, in different situations, manage as such, in its duality, combining two terms – choosing, for example, to be both *exemplary* and *violent* – but that it most often decides in favour of one option or the other.

3. Totality

A communal movement is the more powerful when the individuals who make it up identify intensely with cultural values. The collectivity is directly defined by these values; there is no sense of distance from them, as we have said, and no question of a tension around them or an effort to control or orient them. The actor does not go into action with the aim of directing a historicity which others have appropriated for themselves, others whose domination it could be seen as contesting; it identifies with a historicity which it will not allow to be destroyed or threatened, or which it wants to create or re-create, or wishes to see expand.

What is at issue in the action here is not, then, a set of models or values which the actor might be said to share with its social adversary – as is the case when the labour movement and the bourgeoisie both recognize the positive character of progress and industry and fight over who is to direct it. The aim is to assert one set of models or values against another set, to fight one historicity with another, though this does not exclude borrowings or syncretic formulas in which, for example, the communal movement seeks to assert its religion, derive authority from its own myths, defend its conceptions of politics and social life, at the same time as it appropriates elements of another religion, modes of knowledge or a conception of science and progress which come to it from outside.

In the same way, then, as a communal movement defines itself by a duality with regard to what it opposes, we may speak also of a dualization or a fragmentation where the highest goals of its action are concerned. On the one hand, it is a question of rejecting values, models and an historicity with which the actor refuses to identify and, on the other, of reinforcing its own values, models and historicity and, in some cases, also inventing them. This explains the degree of effort often deployed in community-based struggles not only to draw sustenance from traditions and valorize them, but also to reconstruct a more or less mythic history, recover a disappearing language or promote a form of education specific to the community. From the moment there is no longer a set of values shared with the enemy, but an opposition between two systems of values, the actor can be defined only by the dual tension in which the rejection of the historicity of the Other and the affirmation of its own historicity take place.

4. Communal fusion

It is, in fact, difficult to separate, even analytically, the three principles which have just been separately presented. In a communal movement, these three principles often seem, in effect, to be a single one, so much does each seem to be merely a particular way of accounting for a highly unified reality.

The identity of the actor is given by its convictions, its values, its traditions, its myths: it is the essence of a collective being, which is simply the purpose for which it acts [ce pour quoi il agit]. And that identity soon merges with the object of the action: the actor is in itself the meaning of the action; it is hardly distanced at all from the historicity which orients that action. That is why sometimes, in extreme cases, it presents an image of fundamentalism [intégrisme], of unbending adherence, without any possibility of compromise, to the tradition, values and basic tenets in the name of which it acts.

Similarly, the opponent or, rather, the enemy – or, merely, the Other – is first and foremost what poses a threat or destroys, or what prevents the actor from creating or fulfilling itself in its being and historicity; it is what imposes or introduces another identity, which is something that negates its being. This is why, again in extreme cases, the actor may seem fanatical, prepared to go to any lengths in a battle where it is not just its capacity to produce its existence and give it meaning that is at stake, but, once again, that existence itself, its collective being.

Contrary to what might be said of social movements, it is not, then, possible to speak here of integration of the three elements which define action. These elements cross-refer endlessly to one another and might more accurately be described as fused rather than integrated. Hence the non-negotiable, implacable character of the demands formulated by communal action, which – much more than other types of action – engages in ruthless battles, frequently breaks off all relations and refuses to communicate with the Other, and also issues calls for purity and rejections of compromise. If there is something absolute about these communal movements, if they seem to be based, to such an enormous extent, on strong affects – the emotional community Max Weber speaks of – if they seem to involve such an intense symbiotic relationship with the leaders, this is also because, in the case of these movements, the principles of identity, opposition and totality form – or tend to form – a single whole.

3. The formation of communal movements

Racism is often present within communal movements and, at times, that presence is a very considerable one. It may sometimes be found in their weakest, most diffuse forms, as, for example, where a national conscious-ness only gives rise to a limited degree of action and expresses itself much more in cultural production or at sporting events. It may also be present in the most clear-cut forms of such movements, where, for example, violent and ruptural behaviour mobilizes actors in a sustained, long-term effort. Before examining the relationship between racism and communal move-ments, however, we have to make a number of further points relating to the historical and changing character of these movements.

Whether ethnic, national, religious or based in some other form of community, communal consciousness is not something running changeless throughout history. Traditions, religions, even languages, and the repre-sentation of the past are not eternal and are the product of a work of elaboration and re-elaboration which is constantly being carried on by specific agents – scholars, political activists, prophets, intellectuals – and the role of these agents is crucial whenever it comes to translating consciousness into action. Communal movements – at least in the modern world – are something produced, and not simply reproduced; they arise out of processes of formation and transformation; they displace and represent collectivities which it is not possible to reduce once and for all to a stabilized image. Five types of process most clearly deserve our attention here, so much are they associated, in history, with more or less marked expressions of racism.

1. Defence of the community

When they affect traditional communities, periods of historical change do not leave those communities indifferent or passive and may generate defensive behaviour on their part. On a world scale, colonial conquest is a phenomenon which has given rise to a great variety of forms of resistance.

In a more limited way, the transition from pre-industrial to industrial economies, by destroying earlier forms of sociality, has also led to defensive behaviour, even in the most central societies. In this case, arguments based on tradition, way of life and the identity threatened by modernization have most often been advanced by those most directly affected by the change: the old élites, the notables, property owners, churchmen, etc., who see their ascendancy or power being destabilized and even overturned and become the most active mouthpieces of the appeal to a collective identity. Where modernization is driven by foreign élites, or merely by élites belonging to a minority religion, that appeal may carry a charge of resurgent nationalism and, at the same time, of xenophobia or racism. Thus, for example, in the late nineteenth century, the industrialization of Poland, which had been sliced up between Russia, Prussia and Austria, was to a large extent the work of Germans and Jews, a fact which led to the rise of a very reactionary, anti-urban and anti-semitic nationalism, nostalgic for the pre-industrial era, the most active agents of which were the traditional Polish élites, sections of the nobility, the clergy and the intelligentsia.[13]

By the same token, an industrial crisis or the demise of local industries may also lead to community-wide defensive behaviour, as is seen wherever a single industry which provided a living for a whole town or region goes into total or partial liquidation. Factory closures do not just mean economic difficulties, but the destruction of a community. Such closures give rise to what may be very violent reactions in which an entire collectivity sees not only their wives – who are a central figure in many community struggles – but also other economic actors – networks of local worthies, teachers, etc. – mobilizing around the workers.[14] In these conditions, this mobilization may reactivate earlier forms of racism, such as, for example, an old local fund of anti-Jewish or anti-semitic sentiment, or may create a xenophobic and incipiently racist hardening of feeling directed largely against foreigners who have been brought in at an earlier period (particularly if that period is a recent one) to meet the need for labour.

2. War and conquest

In a stimulating article, Anthony D. Smith rightly calls for the traditional perspective in which war and conquest are explained by the rise of ethnicism and nationalism to be supplemented by a reversal of its terms.[15] From this new point of view, communal consciousness is seen to be shaped by external conflict and territorial expansion, which act as a catalyst to collective cohesion and accelerate or reinforce it. The dynamic to which these phenomena give rise, in which military élites play a crucial role, fires a sense of belonging and identity, bringing in individuals and groups who previously had little feeling of this kind, and mobilizes scientists, technicians, industrialists, workers, peasants and soldiers in a united effort; it transforms traits which were previously not conscious or highly developed – language, historical references and traditions – into tools of collective action. War and conquest disseminate a strong, robust image of the community, provide coherent frames of thought which dissolve the previous, more fragmented ones of many of the participants in the action; they shape and orient communal movements just as much as – if not indeed more than – they arise out of them.

In support of his argument, Smith draws on a range of examples from Antiquity, the French Revolution and the directly ensuing period which he terms that of 'ethnic revival', and also examines this century's two world wars. But it is certainly just as clear that the most extensive military operations of the 1980s in each case exacerbated national or religious sentiments, boosting Argentinian nationalism, for example, and also its British equivalent, in the so-called 'Malvinas/Falklands' war – which injected new political life into the Thatcherite Right – or, in the case of the Iran–Iraq conflict, mobilizing Iran around both the nation and its religion, playing a part in the revival of an Arab nationalism which had been in considerable disarray since the failure of Nasser, and even contributing to an attempt, with Saddam Hussein and the annexation of Kuwait by Iraq in August 1990, to articulate that nationalism to a conquering Islam which had until then seemed more closely associated with the decline of the Arab cause.

The perspective presented here by Smith lies within an intellectual tradition which includes many other thinkers who, each in their own way, stressed the role of conflict in the production of the actors themselves. We may cite Georg Simmel, who saw conflict as a mode of sociation and intensification of the cohesion of the groups involved; Georges Sorel, who advocated class violence which he regarded as a necessary condition for the vitality both of the proletariat and the bourgeoisie; or Frantz Fanon, who viewed violent rupture as the very key to national (if not, indeed, racial) unification of the colonial actor in his or her liberation struggle.[16] So far as racism is concerned, when it issues in conquest or warfare, communal action produces three consequences. First, it does not exclude either of the two fundamental forms of racism (the partial and the total) in offensive, expansionist situations – particularly in colonial expansion. As Memmi explains, for example, 'the boundary-line between colonization and collective assassination is set by the needs of the colonizer. The first European immigrants to the Americas decimated the Indians because they could not use them. Later, to meet the needs of the plantations, they called on black labour and workers imported from Europe.'[17] Secondly, such action favours a differentialist logic and a total racism as soon as it becomes subject more to a logic of war than to one of economic development and expansion. Thirdly, the scope for inegalitarian racism narrows in time of war within the society concerned, insofar as previously racialized groups are either transformed into scapegoats and treated in terms of a differentialist logic or are incorporated into the collectivity much more than they were before. Thus, by drafting blacks into the American army or troops from the Maghreb and other parts of Africa into French ranks, the first and second world wars produced considerable shifts in attitudes both in the USA and in France and its colonies.

3. The crisis of the state and the rise of community

One or more communal movements may form and become active in situations where several communities, previously combined within a single political unit, have ceased to accept their integration and are demanding either a new deal – a different distribution of power, for example – or that the association be dissolved.

Such a situation may be explained in several ways. In a particular case the determining factor might be a crisis of the state which had, up to that point, been capable of managing the pluri-communal society. Lebanon provides a good recent example of this. The Lebanese state, born out of the 'National Pact' of 1943, disintegrated at a gathering pace from the mid-1970s onwards, and, as that structure collapsed, the country's various religious communities could be seen to transform themselves more or less actively into militarized actors and to engage in conflicts which were not only inter- but intra-communal. Here the action and, more precisely, the violence seem to be a product, among other factors, not of purely defensive behaviours or nationalist ideologies, but of deficiencies on the part of the state which open up a space for confrontations in which each community, in spite of undergoing intense transformations, both defends its territories and yet seeks also to exert influence on the political life of the country, the region and even, in some cases, the whole world. Thus, Shi'ite communal violence in particular – and this includes its terrorist manifestations – has unfolded in the vacuum created by the crisis of the state with the aim of asserting a number of things simultaneously: an attachment to a religion, moral precepts, an often frenzied desire to break with the West and a concern to exert greater influence on the destiny of the country and the region.[18]

Barbarous and deadly as it may have been, the Lebanese experience has barely been marked by racism. By contrast, other situations in which the state and the political system are in crisis or their structures are collapsing often lead to clashes of unparalleled violence in which the groups involved define themselves by an ethnic, tribal or clan hostility very close to racial hatred. A substantial part of the history of post-colonial Africa has consisted in this kind of violence, all the more unrestrained for tending towards naked tribalism – untheorized and unideologized – which is what remains when there is no longer any other signification for action.

4. From one communal movement to another

Only very exceptionally do communal movements follow a linear trajectory in which their intensity or their mobilizing force might alone be said to change. Their contents and the significations and orientations to which they give form also vary, to the point where, rather than being merely small inflections, these changes sometimes represent such a substantial reorientation that we may speak of a mutation or the engendering of new communal movements.

This can be clearly seen if we take the Arab world as an example. The 1960s saw the emergence of an Arab nationalism with Nasser as its figurehead, but this was considerably weakened after the defeat which followed the Six Day War of 1967. This weakening of the movement provided the opportunity for Palestinian nationalism to assert itself and advance its own project, which consisted in overturning the order of subordination: for Yasser Arafat, the Palestinian cause could not pin all its hopes on the success of Arab nationalism; in his view, indeed, that nationalism had to place itself in the service of the liberation of Palestine. From the 1970s onwards, the crisis of Arab nationalism – and also the difficulties of the Palestinian movement – contributed to opening up a space, among the same actors, for action to be given a new signification. That signification was now religious in nature, and its vehicle was an – often radical – Islamism, destabilizing the Palestinian movement and moving away, if only in the case of pro-Iranian Shi'ite Islam, from Arab nationalism. In many cases, it was the same people who agitated for the Arab cause in the late 1960s, then for the Palestinian revolution and, subsequently, fought in the name of Islam within the Palestinian movement or in groups like Hezbollah.

In some experiences, then, new identities intervene to inflect the action of the same individuals and come sufficiently into conflict with the old ones for this to result in internal tensions, splits and the appearance of new organizations. In others, and sometimes within the same experiences, contrary syncretistic phenomena are at work, or there is, at least, an effort to integrate significations arising out of different identities.

A communal struggle may very well have within it, for example, a conglomeration of ethnic and national significations. Thus, for example, rather than asking whether the Mau-Mau revolt in Kenya or the Frolinat rebellion in Chad are ethnic or national in character, Robert Brijtenhuijt suggests that such struggles are in fact both at once, a fact which finds expression in a discrepancy between nationalist objectives and an ethnically or regionally based mobilization.[19] Similarly, it has often been observed that nationalism can be built by a process of absorbing or even crushing previously existing communities: for example, Ernest Gellner notes that 'pre-nationalist Germany was made up of a multiplicity of genuine communities, many of them rural. Post-nationalist united Germany was mainly industrial and a mass society.'[20] Similar observations could be made in the case of France, which only really came into being with the Third Republic and its education system, and with the mass mobilization of the First World War.

This work on meaning, these reorientations – which we have presented here very rapidly and superficially – attest to the existence of an important phenomenon. Communal movements are always likely to produce or appropriate new referents of identity [*référents identitaires*], if not indeed to generate new communal actors, other than themselves; they are always likely to create or take up a meaning which substantially displaces their action. It is, therefore, very hazardous to seek to reduce that action – as writers like Edward Shils or Clifford Geertz do – to a stable body of traditions or the idea of primordial values.[21] This is why it is generally insufficient, and sometimes even wrong, to explain communal action in terms of a culture, a religion, a past history, or more or less biological characteristics which could be said to lay down the actor's orientations once and for all and shape its propensity to violence, exemplary action or any other kind of conduct.

This is also why the place of racism as a signification of action in communal movements cannot be regarded as stable and fixed once and for all, and why it is always susceptible of considerable variations. We shall return to this point later, though we shall provide one example here to illustrate it – that of the Basque movement. At its formation, and for quite some time after the period in which it was led by its main founder, Sabino Arana, Basque nationalism contained a secondary, but quite real, racist dimension, with the affirmation of the existence of a Basque race and, consequently, of other races. The considerable crisis which the survival of the Franco dictatorship beyond the Second World War produced within that movement led to the emergence of a new actor, the ETA movement, and the abandonment, both in that movement and within traditional Basque nationalism, of its racialist thematics. Racism, as can be seen from the Basque experience, may certainly disappear from the consciousness of the communal actor; on the other hand, it may also assert itself within that consciousness, as part of its development. There is, then, no automatic relationship between communal movements and racism.

5. Communal movements and social movements

If we have to distinguish analytically between social and communal movements, we also have to consider the historical connections which cause them, in many concrete historical experiences, to act as prolongations one of the other. The formation of a social movement, like its decline, is a long, chaotic process in which actions of a communal type have an important place, in both the initial and final phases.

Thus, in his famous book on the formation of the English working class, Edward P. Thompson shows how working-class consciousness is forged over a long process, the first important phases of which fall within the ambit of communal movements. In the beginning, the English labour movement existed among Dissenters, in Methodism, the millennarian movement or 'the dark Satanic mills', in the formation of various communities or even in the maintenance of pre-industrial values and traditions.[22] Similarly, the first waves which, from the 1970s onwards, heralded the birth of new social movements in many of the countries of the Western world were, broadly speaking, very strongly identity-based. The women's movement, notes Alain Touraine, 'begins with a defensive appeal to identity, difference, specificity, and community',[23] and even passes through extreme forms of quasi-sectarian closure; the ecological movement is based to a large extent on the defence of local communities, resistance to industrialization, the fear of damage to the environment and threats to life and to health. It too has often closed itself off in sectarianism and an identity-based rejectionist attitude. We may, however, take the view that this represents a – pre-social – moment in which a properly social conflict is emerging, but the actors in that conflict are merely temporarily unable to recognize its terms and determine who are their adversaries.

By the same token, the decline of a social movement provides a favourable terrain for the formation or reinforcement of communal movements. We see this in contemporary France, where the exhaustion of the labour movement has helped to produce an upsurge of all kinds of identity-based demands, whether religious, ethnic or nationalist in nature. It can also be seen in many other situations, such as the transformation of student movements into religious movements – as in Egypt in the late 1960s[24] – or in the degeneration of peasant or proletarian movements into essentially community-based action, as was the case in Lebanon with Hezbollah, which has become simultaneously religious, violent and exemplary of a struggle which, twenty years earlier, spoke in the name of the 'have-nots' and was, at that point, something akin to a social movement.[25]

With these remarks, we come to a crucial point, which the reader will perhaps already have gleaned from the preceding pages. The notion of a communal movement is in many respects similar to that of a social anti-movement, to the point that it may be substituted for it in the case of those communal forms just mentioned which are linked to the formation and decline of social movements. This is why the analyses we have proposed with regard to social anti-movements may also, to a great degree, be applied to communal movements, which always constitute a favourable space for the spread of racism. Once again, however, let us not deduce too quickly from this proposition the idea that there is a direct link between awareness of a separate identity [*conscience identitaire*] and racism: the problem is more complex than this.

4. Racism and Identity

That there should be a potential for racism within communal phenomena is not surprising. The more these latter propose a strong, totalizing orientation, the more, to use Allport's terms, they separate 'ingroups' and 'outgroups', and the more, also, they appeal to ideas of difference and rupture, then the more the reference points they offer propel the collectivity, or certain of its members, into a non-social universe which leaves room for mysticism and for biological or physical definitions of the self and the Other. In communal movements, the field of consciousness and action is barely conceived within a social framework at all. Identity is not defined in terms of a relation, nor even less of a structural position within a relationship of domination. That identity situates the actor in history and, ultimately, in the cosmos, and this is something which encourages the naturalizing or demonizing of the Other, the valorization of genealogy, of kinship, the obsessive fear of interbreeding or appeals to racial community.

This is why extreme positions, particularly those of a Marxist inclination, which deny the connection between racism and communal action, are very marginal and generally unconvincing, as is illustrated by Paul Gilroy's criticism of Benedict Anderson, for whom 'the dreams of racism actually have their origin in ideologies of *class*, rather than in those of nation'.[26]

Racism in the strict biological or physical sense often seems to have its place in communal movements, either as something latent and marginal or as a visible and central feature. And it has a very particular place which means that it cannot just be treated as one identity-based signification among others. It sometimes seems hemmed in by other identities, surrounded by references which each constitute concentric envelopes more or less resistant to its deployment. But also, at times, like the seed within a fruit, it seems capable of bursting out on its own, of becoming the main mobilizing force and going on from there to orient and transform the other – cultural, religious and historical – elements of identity. Étienne Balibar has clearly shown how, at one and the same time, racism is part of the communal phenomenon and stands in a remarkable relation to it. What he says of nationalism may be extended to other principles of identity: 'racism is not an "expression" of nationalism, but *a supplement of nationalism* or more precisely *a supplement internal to nationalism*, always in excess of it, but always indispensable to its constitution and yet still insufficient to achieve its project'.[27] Similarly, Balibar has pointed out how the rise of racism within a communal movement, especially within nationalism, brings about substantial changes and affects all the other elements of identity: 'By seeking to circumscribe the common essence of nationals, racism thus inevitably becomes involved in the obsessional quest for a "core" of authenticity that cannot be found, shrinks the category of nationality and de-stabilizes the historical nation.'[28]

Racism is not reducible to communal action and many experiences which form part of the immense body of communal actions are totally free from it, which means that too direct or inescapable a connection should not be drawn between a particular form of communal action – most importantly, nationalism – and racism.[29] And when this latter is present, it is so in forms which arise out of distinct processes. In some cases the formation of a communal identity includes racist significations from the outset, and implies within it a more or less explicit project to set apart or subordinate a racialized group; it brings together racist sentiments and affects which are more or less widely disseminated within the collectivity, forges these into an ethnic, national or religious consciousness and the whole acquires a mobilizing force which owes a great deal to the intervention of political agents, doctrinarians and ideologues, and élites which establish a foothold for this action at the political level. In other cases, by contrast, whatever forms it takes, racism only makes its appearance as the movement evolves, or as it is coming to an end, when other identity-based referents enter into crisis or are weakened, as though it formed a hard core which crystallizes only when other elements of meaning have been exhausted. We can, in fact, identify two orientations within these processes.

5. The two orientations of identity-based racism

The first of these is that of failure, impotence, adversity and fear, an orientation which causes a national or religious identity to harden, contract and tighten around a racial principle and be translated into a frenzied quest for scapegoats. The second is an expansive, affirmative, conquering, dominating orientation, which makes racism the engine of action, or at least its justification. These two orientations may be present in succession and may even give rise to a genuine spiralling interaction. Thus, for example, in the beginning, the Nazi experience arose out of the national humiliation which followed the defeat of 1918 (among other things), but at a very early stage anti-semitism became a mobilizing force, with the Jews no longer merely as a scapegoat, but as the absolute embodiment of evil and the enemy. Yet we must, none the less, add that in this precise case anti-semitism did not increase with the Nazi seizure of power and that it was only for Germany's rulers that it constituted the horizon of their action.

Most importantly, it is possible for these two orientations, by virtue of which racism is able to find a space both in the crisis of a communal movement and in its expansion, to intersect without being mutually destructive, and they may even feed on one another. Thus, for example, the purity of blood laws in fifteenth-century Spain developed initially against a background of *reconquista* and religious zeal, at the point when the government was first embarking on its colonial adventure; but if those laws remained in force until the mid-nineteenth century, then, as Charles Amiel very clearly shows, they did so – against a background of societal mutation – as a result of the difficulties encountered by all kinds of social groups which, when confronted with the rise of the 'neo-Christians', came together in a common hostility to forge an anxious collectivity governed not merely by 'a concern for wealth, but by an obsession with social status'.[30]

Racism here is the child – and the father – of change. It expresses the dramas, the growing tensions and the impotence experienced by a collectivity, as much as it may indicate its capacity for expansion. It provides a resolution for those tensions and dramas and a dynamic for that expansion, and enables the two orientations of crisis and expansion – either of which can take on a differentialist or an inegalitarian form – to be conjoined and even fused.

This distinction between two orientations is an essential point and it enables us to explain the kinds of ambivalence we have already pointed out in pre-war social Darwinism and eugenics and to draw a demarcation line within racial thinking between theorists like Gobineau, who are over-whelmingly obsessed with decline and decadence, and others, like Chamberlain, who are more optimistic or counter-offensive and capable of looking to the future with a degree of confidence. That distinction also provides a decisive key for the analysis of certain historical experiences, as can be seen from Robert O. Paxton and Michael Marrus's work on Vichy and the Jews.[31] The central idea of these authors can, in fact, be summed up in their theory of the three concentric circles: the outer circle represents a diffuse area of vague, moderate anti-Jewish sentiments; the middle circle is the site of more intense and unstable feelings and reactions, forming a defensive zone which grows in times of unrest; the central core is made up of a fanatical, obsessional anti-semitism, exhorting others to action and the celebration of their own race. Paxton and Marrus's second and third circles correspond quite closely to our two orientations of communal racism – the orientations of crisis and expansion – and the great virtue of their study is that it shows how the worst scenario develops when everything comes together, as was the case with German Nazism, and also with Vichy France, and with the Iron Guard and Arrow Cross movements in Romania and Hungary.[32]

6. Beyond communal movements

Communal consciousness does not necessarily translate itself into action, and, where religious feelings or the sense of belonging to a nation or other collectivity are concerned, it is often excessive to speak in terms of a movement. Can the ideas proposed here be applied to the diffuse and less active forms of communal consciousness? We shall give a nuanced answer to this question, and one which requires that we first distinguish between the study of individuals or groups external to a constituted communal movement, but operating in a situation in which that movement plays an important role, and situations where only a small part – or no part at all – is played by a movement properly so-called.

In the first case, communal identity provides reference points, a mode of structuring the social imaginary and a basis for cognitive processes or representations which exert a force of attraction that reaches far beyond the mere actors involved or their sympathizers. That identity constitutes a visible, available site of meaning which gives – or restores – a legitimacy to

individual and collective experience; it provides a principle of identification, and also grants authority to think and act in terms of its categories;
it removes moral or political prohibitions; and it paralyses opponents.
Those who take up their positions with regard to the markers that identity
puts down are not wholly and solely those who give form to those markers
or who seek directly to translate them into action; these people follow their
development at a greater or lesser remove and are affected by the same
orientations of racism – in its crisis or expansion-related forms – but less
distinctly, with possibly a degree of excess or shortfall.

In the second case, the consciousness of belonging to a community is less
active and also less structured, not being so clearly directed by specific
agents capable of shaping it. It is at the mercy of developments which
mould or transform it – political, inter-communal, demographic and social
changes – and the markers it creates for itself are hazier. Both orientations
of racism find limited scope here, this terrain being favourable to a
fragmented racism and actions of no great scale or stability, or to the
expression of prejudices relatively unconnected with any concrete practice.
Most importantly, we can say that there is more scope here for the
orientation towards a racism of crisis and loss of meaning than for an
expansion-related racism, the dynamic of which calls at an early stage for
transition to the political sphere and the development there of a specific
action.

Even in this case, however, it seems to us that we have to maintain what
has been our attitude throughout: the idea that what is in play here is a
relation between two types of action, weak as these may seem – that is to
say, a relation between a fragmented racism and a communal consciousness – not between the two objectivized categories of race and community.

CONCLUSION:
THE UNITY OF RACISM

The time has come to give our answer to a crucial question: is there a unity to racism, and, if so, what does it consist in?

We began this book by examining the various approaches to the phenomenon and our analysis of the main currents of thinking quite clearly provided only a negative response to this question. Most of the time, however, the question is not asked and the argument only covers, more or less satisfactorily, certain historical experiences or some aspects of these.

The distinctions we subsequently introduced enable us to investigate the elementary forms of racism, but lead more to the elaboration of typologies than to the creation of any image of unity. They specify the differences in the logics and levels of hatred, contempt or persecution, without providing any sense of what permits us to conceive these in their totality.

Lastly, in distinguishing between the social sources, on the one hand, and the communal sources, on the other, from which the space of racism is liable to expand, we have also not been proposing a unified image of the phenomenon.

But it is not possible to leave matters there.

I

To begin with, let us look once again at each of the two fundamental logics of racism. As we have observed throughout, these are constantly intersecting, cross-referring and merging into one another whenever the experience in question assumes any degree of historical importance. Inferiorization leads to exclusion, and vice versa. Even in the Nazi experience, the logic of exclusion and destruction, which was the most decisive, did not prevent efforts also being made, to the very end, to use Jews as labour, and the relative position such a logic occupied at different stages is a central issue in the historiographical debates which have recently been given new impetus in France by the translation of Arno Mayer's work *Why Did the Heavens Not Darken? The 'Final Solution' in History*.[1]

Though we have to make an analytical distinction between inferiorization and differentiation, we also have to take into account the fact that racism only unfolds in reality through a combination of the two, with a simultaneous reference – contradictory as this might seem – to a difference and an inequality, and a necessary and, more or less, irresolvable tension between the call to divide the social body and the call to unite it.

We may come upon exclusively inegalitarian or exclusively differentialist logics in the writings of theorists and ideologues, but, as soon as racism becomes practical, as soon as it is given concrete expression, whether this is limited to opinions and prejudices or much more active, it leads either to the combination of the two principles or, in its most extreme developments, to behaviour and situations which move us away from a biologically inflected definition of the Other.

If it is able to base itself on their phenotype or on a definition of a racist kind, the inferiorization of the most deprived leads either to forms of racial segregation – and therefore of differentiation – or to an exclusion in which the most decisive aspects are social and economic, not racial, in nature. The great strength of the arguments of William J. Wilson and the British and American 'underclass' analysts lies in their having shown how, for large masses of people, the black problem (and not only that problem) has become one of poverty, of non-participation and social sidelining, much more than a problem of racism properly so-called.

Similarly, the differentialist rejection of the Other – setting him apart or engaging in armed conflict with him – have little or no need of a biological thematics for their development: cultural rejection and nationalistic self-affirmation are quite sufficient. The Other has to be at least minimally present socially and economically, and there thus has to be some connection – albeit a weak or even mythical one – with a principle of inequality if the assertion of a communal identity is to veer off into a process of racialization. In itself, as Claude Lévi-Strauss asserted in his famous 1971 lecture, there is no inherent danger in the recognition of the diversity of cultures; it is when this gives way to the assertion of their inequality that racism arises, this latter being indissociable from the sense of a superiority based on relations of domination.

This is why it seems to us possible to assert the theoretical unity of racism, in spite of its great practical heterogeneity: racism is a mode of management of two principles (inferiorization and differentiation) and its various concrete expressions are merely so many distinct modalities of a biologization which resolves the tension or contradiction between these two principles. When that tension is weak, the forms of racism are themselves partial or debased; when it is strong, we come close to a total, fused racism; and where the phenomenon is dominated either by the one or the other of our two principles, this is because it lies within configurations where either the social question or the national (or, more broadly, communal) question assumes the greater importance.

II

A complementary examination of the social and communal processes which govern the expansion of the scope of racism will enable us to provide more detailed grounds for this affirmation of the theoretical unity of the phenomenon. For reasons which are, here again, analytical, we have made a clear distinction between the register of social transformations and that of the mechanisms involved in a centring on community or in the upsurge of communal sentiment: we now have to show that these two registers are not totally independent and that it is a feature of our societies that we seek constantly to combine them, with greater or lesser degrees of success.

This idea may be formulated, first of all, in terms still quite close to those we have employed so far, by our noting the correlation between the destructuring of social movements and the expansion of communal phenomena.

Over the last twenty years or so, we have seen an irreversible decline of the labour movement in many countries, accompanied by a return of ethnicity, the affirmation of religious convictions, and the assertion of refound, renewed or reinforced identities – mainly national, religious and cultural in form. The social crisis in these countries has led to non-social identities acquiring increased importance, and a country like France is not the only one where the dominance of the social question has given way to the dominance of issues around the nation. There is a certain unity to these two orders of problem, since what happens in the one register is shaped to a considerable degree by what takes place in the other.

It is this painful mutation, in which the two registers seem to comple-ment each other in an unbalanced way – in the contraction of social action and the reinforcement of communal action – which constitutes the drama of our present societies. And if racism seems to pose a more real threat now than it did ten or twenty years ago, this is because, among other phenomena, it is an expression of a development in which our societies are not only swinging over from the one register to the other, but are also becoming less capable than before of keeping the two registers integrated. France is an exemplary case here. First, the collapse of the labour movement has cleared the way for a society tending towards dualization, with, on the one hand, the social outcasts and the others left behind by social change, and, on the other, the great mass of those who, in the middle and working classes, still have jobs, are consumers and have not been dragged down in the decline. Secondly, the theme of the nation now occupies a central place, together with the themes of religion and culture – if only reactively, in response to Islam having become the country's second largest religion. It is patently obvious that this development destabilizes the classic model – a model asserted with particular vigour since the Third Republic – of a Republican, secular France, a national society in which the state could both embody the nation and play the role of managing an industrial society.[2]

But let us formulate this problem in a more general way. In a sense, the labour movement as we have defined it – as a social movement engaged in a struggle for the control of progress – is merely one figure of modernity, one illustration among others of our societies' identification with reason and universalism. Within this perspective, the destructuring of that movement may seem like one of the expressions of the crisis of modernity; racism, then, becomes the product of the conjunction of this crisis of modernity with the increasing difficulty of combining the faltering values of progress and reason with a communal and, particularly, national consciousness. This allows us to broaden our perspective to those societies the world over which, though not having known true social movements, have sought to identify with progress, reason and a universalism inherited from the Enlightenment (including societies where this has occurred in the form of revolutionary or Marxist ideologies). And this, in particular, leads us to see the unity of racism, once and for all, in terms of the dissociation it expresses between modernity and the particularism of the nation or, more broadly, of the community. Racism develops where reason and nation, universal values and the reference to a specificity cannot be integrated or where they are disintegrating; it finds its own particular space in the gap which opens up between these two registers and in the effort to bridge that gap in tendentially biological terms.

III

On the basis of such a definition, it becomes possible to propose a typology of racism which distinguishes between three main scenarios, three particular modalities of this phenomenon of disjunction between modernity and the appeal to communal values.

The first of these is the case where universalist values win out and, instead of combining with particularist values – national ones, for example – combat and deny them. In this perspective, racism functions to naturalize everything which is not identified with modernity or resists it or is slow to participate in it. It is an expression of triumphant modernity, as, for example, when that modernity embarks upon colonial ventures and, more particularly, when it develops relations of colonial domination. It is then the property of economic, political and even religious élites, and is not, to any great extent, disseminated among the general populace.

The second scenario is symmetrical with this first one. Here a group feels so threatened or uprooted by modernity that it rejects and resists it. In this case, racism is an expression of a particularism in the face of the universal values of modernity, which are then identified with a group which comes evilly to symbolize them. For a century now, the Jew has been constantly portrayed as the embodiment of that destructive, anonymous, cosmopolitan, rootless modernity, even if anti-semitism also at times prefers to attack the Jews in their most traditional, most visible features. Let us add that, here, the racism is socially indeterminate and may be an attribute both of lower-class actors and of élites.

Lastly, a third scenario is provided by intermediate situations, in which the racializing group does not go over distinctly either to universalism or particularism, but is, rather, defined by a process which tends to exclude it from a modernity with which it does not, in fact, wish to break. Here the racist actor loses his social bearings or is in danger of losing them; he is afraid of dropping down the social ladder, and of having his social identity, his sense of belonging to the modern world – the world of work and employment, production and consumption – denied, and falls back on other communal or biological markers. In this lurching movement, racism assumes the features of a perverted social relation which seeks to inferiorize the Other at the same time as it tends to exclude or destroy him; this racism is the preserve of lower-class actors operating on the 'poor white' model. The rejection of black proletarians by white workers, the 'northern-style' riots Grimshaw speaks of, are variants of this scenario.

These three scenarios can be ranked hierarchically. Not so as in some way to establish gradations of contemptibility, but because they correspond to a greater or lesser radicalization of the actors. This is at its most extreme when a particularism stands out against the penetration of modernity or the spread of universal values. It is already less marked where the actor is resisting exclusion from the field of modernity and fighting social decline and where he takes up a position around communal markers, without these latter constituting his entire horizon. The radicalization is even less pronounced when the universalism of reason and progress predominates, as it did in the colonial racism of the French Third Republic, which saw it as its mission to 'civilize the inferior races', as Jules Ferry put it, and thus to deliver them from their state of nature.[3]

It thus seems possible for us to assert, once and for all, the unity of racism. This follows from the necessary combination of its two basic logics – of inferiorization and differentiation – and, also, from the disjunction between universalist references and particularist values.

CONCLUSION

The analysis of the conditions under which racism spreads certainly leaves many aspects of the phenomenon – perhaps, even, the most disturbing ones – in obscurity. It tells us little about the anthropological nature of the evil, which shows up here more as a potentiality than in its most profound foundations, though whether those foundations can, in fact, be referred to some kind of – individual or collective – human invariant is not clear. It refuses to portray racism as an attribute of certain cultures, societies or religions, as is done, for example, when Catholicism is credited with a different role from Protestantism in establishing colonial racism. And it seems to situate the phenomenon within a short-run time-scale – in phases of societal mutation or in the transformations a communal consciousness undergoes – leaving out of account that remarkable 'density' of history which confers both their permanence and some measure of their dynamism on many historical experiences.

These limits – and we have certainly not provided an exhaustive list of them here – in fact mark out the space of a sociology of racism. Racism is an *action*, with its elementary forms, its representations, its active behaviours, its political expressions, its modes of mobilization; and also with its history, its 'grand narratives', its memory, its varying purchase on different periods and societies, its inflections or fluctuations, its leaders and doctrinarians, and also its more or less explicitly anti-racist opponents. But, though it is an action, it is not one that can be studied in itself, without taking other actions into consideration. It can, admittedly, be isolated and its specificity must be acknowledged, its elementary forms and specific logics identified; but only in extreme cases, where all other meaning is wiped out, is racism a naked force, a pure signification. Most often, it progresses as a function of two gradients and the combination of the tendencies they represent: it develops as social relations decay or social movements have difficulty forming, as communal action and consciousness undergo change and, more widely, as the two split apart. This is why it seemed right to set it within a triangular field – with racism itself at one apex of that field, social movements at a second, and communal movements at the third – and to examine the principal relationships in play within that properly sociological space.

This is a space we are not the first to construct in this way, since an important intellectual and political tradition moves between the three poles to which we have just referred – race, class and nation, as Balibar and Wallerstein have it, for example, in the joint work quoted above (the title and cover illustration of that book making the point quite clearly).* It is, first and foremost, a space in which we have been able to hone a set of conceptual tools that should enable us to analyse precise experiences of racism.

So we are saying, then, that the spread of racism takes place against a background of the breakdown, absence or inversion of social movements and, more generally, of a crisis of modernity? In that case, let us study the state of social movements, their transformations, their capacity to structure individual and collective behaviour more or less effectively, to provide social bearings and an organizing principle for social life; let us study the crisis of universal values, of reason and the idea of progress. And this crisis is difficult to dissociate from community-based references, appeals to the nation, to religion, to a non-social identity? Let us study, then, the phenomena of the rise or decline of identity-based movements, the shifts within them, the historical or sacred materials on which they draw or which they invent.

And since it has to do, above all, with the dissociation of the social from the communal and, more generally, of the universal from the particular, let us also study the modes of the joint management of meaning, the artificial efforts to associate class and nation, social project and communal aims in patterns like populism; let us study also, and most importantly, the modalities of a racialization which sets its seal on this dissociation.

But let us look back now on what we have argued in this book, first reversing the order of presentation, then running back against the grain of the argument. We are saying, then, that, within the triangle which defines its sociological space, racism does not conform to one single logic; it unfolds along two distinct axes and differs according to whether or not it has established itself at the political level? It can be partial or total – or, to put it another way, predominantly inegalitarian or differentialist? Let us learn, then, how to recognize which of these logics is dominant in a given experience and, especially, how to recognize the modalities of their combination or of the transition from the one to the other. And we are saying that it may be fragmented or tend towards fusion? Let us examine, then, the political conditions for its possible elevation to the political level, the role of the factors producing that elevation, the specific dynamic it creates.

People often ask what the social sciences are for. The answer this book has attempted to provide is a clear one. We did not wish to involve ourselves in the issues of the moment, to harangue anti-racist organizations and activists; still less did we wish to embark on a critique of their action, necessary as this may be in certain respects. It seemed preferable to

---

* *Translator's note*: The reference is to the French edition of *Race, Nation, Class*, where the cover illustration is a grey, Escher-like triangular figure on a blue ground.

develop instruments of analysis capable of offering guidance, in the field, to those who wish to provide precise knowledge of the key processes by which the evil spreads. The value of these instruments lies entirely in the practical results they are able to produce and the additional measure of intelligibility they can contribute when applied to historical realities. Which amounts to saying that this book lays the ground for – and is the precursor to – a research project which is much more concrete in nature.

Are these instruments capable of improving not only our knowledge, but also our action; can they assist in the development of anti-racist policies? A precise answer to this question would require the introduction of new lines of argument, a detailed examination of practices in this area and of the copious literature, particularly of British and American origin, which attests to the diversity of possible actions, at a national or local, general or sectoral level, together with a close look at the controversies which have arisen over means, if not indeed over ends.[1] This would be to go beyond the size and scope of this book.

Yet it seems possible, in conclusion, that we can go beyond well-intentioned, but merely incantatory formulas which simply appeal to reason and ethics as the means to curb racism.

We have just referred once again to the importance of the distinction between two levels – the political and the infra-political – in the analysis of racism. This suggests that the phenomenon can and must be combated by active policies, by legislative and regulatory measures, by efforts which may be direct and explicit but which may also take on the problem indirectly, at times without even referring to it by name – for example, in the form of urban or education policies. But if our analyses are well founded, they also – and, indeed, mainly – represent an invitation to situate thinking on such action at a point before the political system, institutions and the state come into play, and to look, first and foremost, at the state of social relations and communal forces in the societies in question.

If racism is an action which arises out of the weakness of social movements, and out of phenomena associated with the rise of – or a centring upon – community, the latter being themselves conditioned by the former – must we not, then, conclude that everything which reinforces social movements and, more broadly, increases the space for properly social relations cannot but reduce the scope for racism? This hypothesis may seem paradoxical. Have we not, for example, several times traced a connection between racism and the relations of domination which structure American society? The paradox is, in reality, only apparent. The point is clearly not to call for the reinforcement of such relations; it is to argue for the conflictualization, in a social mode, of tensions and difficulties which are too often or too widely lived out in a non-social (particularly communal or racial) mode. As an example to help us illustrate this idea, let us take the question of education in contemporary France. The more the problem of schooling is experienced there as one of immigration or Islam, the more one sees, on the one hand, individual behaviours which establish a *de facto* segregation and, on the other, resentment on the part of those French people 'born and bred' who do not have the means to take their children out of schools with a high proportion of immigrants. And the more one also sees media and politico-ideological explosions like the 'Islamic headscarf' affair, which betray the presence of fear and anxiety, and sometimes also more or less overt racism or xenophobia.[2] Would it not be desirable for the interest here to be shifted more clearly towards debates on the goals of education, towards conflict and protest around what the schools produce, around teaching methods, academic under-achievement, the aims of training or the autonomy of educational establishments?

Michel Crozier has quite properly argued that society is not changed by decree.[3] Nor can one create movements or social relations merely by desiring them. But it is surely clear, none the less, that in a thousand and one situations the problems and tensions which arise – depending on whether they are experienced, conceived and managed in the register of rupture, non-relation and violence or in that of social conflict and negotiation – can very easily play a part either in the production of racism or in action which excludes it as a possibility. And clear also that it very often takes very little – the intervention of a few teachers, a handful of social workers, a neighbourhood association, or a group of trade unionists – for a difficult situation to be modified in one direction or another, for social actors to emerge and assert themselves, or, on the other hand, for tendencies towards anti-movement, communal closure and racism to be reinforced.

Yet we should also not seek over-hastily to counterpose the construction of social relations to the process of becoming centred on an identity. Wherever a sense of community or strong identities exist, it is absurd, artificial and unjust to wish to grind these down in the name of modernity, and the best response to the racist tendencies they may harbour consists, not in rejecting them, but in encouraging everything that makes it possible for them to be tied in to universalist values. Racism, as we have seen, spreads where the social and the communal – and reason and national or religious identity – are disjoined, whereas its scope diminishes when links are created between these two registers. This is why we have to support and be sympathetic to those endeavours in which actors resist that disjunction and attempt to invent formulas of integration in which reference to a collective entity in no way excludes the appeal to progress and the call to participate in modernity.

NOTES

Preface

1. Commission nationale consultative des droits de l'homme, *Rapport au premier ministre sur la lutte contre le racisme et la xénophobie*, Paris, 1989.

2. It should be remembered that at Aix-les-Bains the scandal was provoked in November 1989 by local councillors from the opposition parties, the town's Jews having been criticized for their non-integration into local life and hence their difference and visibility. At Carpentras, tombs in the Jewish cemetery were desecrated in May 1990 and a corpse exhumed and abused.

3. Pierre-André Taguieff, *La Force du préjugé. Essai sur le racisme et ses doubles*, La Découverte, Paris, 1988; Étienne Balibar and Immanuel Wallerstein, *Race, Nation, Class. Ambiguous Identities*, trans. Chris Turner, Verso, London, 1991; Nonna Mayer and Pascal Perrineau (eds), *Le Front national à découvert*, FNSP, Paris, 1989.

4. For a complete overview of the work of Roger Bastide, see 'Roger Bastide. Bibliographie', *Cahiers d'anthropologie*, numéro spécial, 1978; for Albert Memmi, see in particular his *Portrait du colonisé*, Payot, Paris, 1973 and (with P.-H. Maucorps and J.-F. Held), *Les Français et le racisme*, Payot, Paris, 1965; Colette Guillaumin, *L'Idéologie raciste. Genèse et langage actuel*, Mouton, The Hague, 1972.

5. See the overall assessment offered by François Dubet in *Immigrations, qu'en savons-nous? Un bilan des connaissances*, La Documentation française, Paris, 1989.

6. Gunnar Myrdal, *An American Dilemma. The Negro Problem and Modern Democracy*, Harper and Row, New York, 1944, 2 vols.

7. See Didier Lapeyronnie and Marcin Frybes, *L'Intégration des minorités immigrées. Étude comparative France–Grande-Bretagne*, ADRI-BIT, Paris, 1990.

Part One

Introduction

1. Albert Jacquard and J.-B. Pontalis, 'Entretien: une tête qui ne convient pas', *Le Genre humain*, no. 11, 1984–5, p. 15.

2. Gérard Lemaine and Benjamin Matalon, *Hommes supérieurs, Hommes inférieurs? La controverse sur l'hérédité de l'intelligence*, Armand Colin, Paris, 1985.

3. Alain de Benoist, 'Racisme: remarques autour d'une définition', in A. Bégin and J. Freund (eds), *Racismes, Antiracismes*, Klincksieck, Paris, 1986, pp. 203–51.

4. Colette Guillaumin, *L'Idéologie raciste. Genèse et langage actuel*, Mouton, The Hague, 1972, p. 63.

Chapter 1

1. Christian Delacampagne, *L'Invention du racisme*, Fayard, Paris, 1983.

2. See Carl von Linné, *L'Équilibre de la nature*, Vrin, Paris, 1972.

3. There is an interesting discussion of this classificatory thinking in Tzvetan Todorov (*Nous et les Autres*, Éditions du Seuil, Paris, 1989), who looks, among other writers, at Buffon, whose *L'Histoire naturelle* exerted considerable influence and in whose view people, though they belong to one and the same species since they are capable of procreating together, are characterized by differences in which physical features are indissociable from mores or culture. Buffon, notes Todorov, 'considers the existence of races as self-evident, asserts a solidarity between the physical and the moral dimensions and implies that the individual is determined by the group' (p. 126).

4. Gustave Le Bon, *Lois psychologiques de l'évolution des peuples*, Alcan, Paris, 1894.

5. Arthur de Gobineau, *Essai sur l'inégalité des races humaines*, Firmin-Didot, Paris, 1940 (first published in 1852).

6. Georges Vacher de Lapouge, *L'Aryen. Son rôle social*, A. Fontemoing, Paris, 1899.

7. See *The American Journal of Sociology*, which published the text of two of his lectures (vol. X, no. 1, July 1904, pp. 1–25, and vol. XI, no. 1, July 1905, pp. 11–25), together with long extracts from the discussions (vol. XI, no. 1, Sept. 1905). Some were flatly opposed to Galton in these discussions (notably H.G. Wells and Max Nordau); others displayed less resistance: Tönnies expressed some reservations, but took the view overall that 'the first and main point is to secure the general *intellectual* acceptance of eugenics as a hopeful and most important study' (vol. XI, no. 1, p. 292); Bertrand Russell 'agree[d] entirely with the view that marriage customs might be modified in a eugenic direction' (ibid., p. 288).

8. Houston Stewart Chamberlain, *Foundations of the Nineteenth Century* (2 vols), trans. John Lees, John Lane, London, 1910 (first published in 1902).

9. See Michael Graetz, *Les Juifs en France au XIXᵉ siècle*, Éditions du Seuil, Paris, 1989, pp. 352–3 (first published, in Hebrew, by the Bialack Institute, Jerusalem, 1982). On the eve of the Second World War, one still finds Jewish intellectuals expounding racist thinking relative to the Jews. This is the case, in particular, with the Zionist Arthur Ruppin, who worked as a demographer for the Jewish Agency in Palestine, and who resorted to physical anthropology to define a non-religious Jewish identity; see his *Les Juifs dans le monde moderne*, Payot, Paris, 1934, and, on the person of the author, see Jacob Katz, 'Misreading of Anti-Semitism', *Commentary*, no. 76, July 1983, pp. 39–44. Let us add – and this is an immense problem – that the very way in which Jews most often conceive the transmission of Jewishness (through the mother) is biological in nature.

10. See, for example, Stephen Jay Gould, *The Mismeasure of Man*, W.W. Norton, New York, 1981; Michael Banton, *The Idea of Race, Tavistock, London, 1977, and Racial Theories*, Cambridge University Press, Cambridge, 1987; Léon Poliakov, *The History of Anti-Semitism* (vols 1–3), Routledge and Kegan Paul, London, 1974–5 (vol. 4, Oxford University Press, Oxford, 1985). (Vol. 1, trans. Richard Howard, first published in 1965 by Vanguard Press, New York, and in 1966 by Elek, London; vol. 2, trans. Natalie Gerardi, first published in 1973 by Vanguard Press, London; vol. 3, trans. Miriam Kachan; and vol. 4, trans. G. Klin for the Littman Library of Jewish Civilization, Oxford.) See also, on many of these matters, Pierre-André Taguieff, *La Force du préjugé. Essai sur le racisme et ses doubles*, La Découverte, Paris, 1988. For a well-documented version which is very close to the current arguments of the extreme Right, see Jean-Pierre Hébert, *Race et intelligence*, Copernic, Paris, 1977.

11. See, for example, Utz Seggle, 'L'ethnologie de l'Allemagne sous le régime nazi', *Ethnologie française*, no. 2, 1988, pp. 114–19; and, in the same number, Édouard Conte, 'Le confesseur du dernier Habsbourg et les nouveaux païens allemands. A propos de Wilhelm Schmidt', pp. 120–30. On medicine, see Robert Jay Lifton, *The Nazi Doctors*, Basic Books, New York, 1986; and Benno Müller-Hill, *Murderous Science. Elimination by Scientific Selection of Jews, Gypsies, and Others, Germany 1933–45*, trans. George R. Fraser, Oxford University Press, Oxford/New York/Tokyo, 1988.

12. On archaeology, see Alain Schnapp, 'Archéologie, archéologues et nazisme', in Maurice Olender (ed.), *Le Racisme. Mythes et sciences*, Complexe, Brussels, 1981, pp. 289–316 and Schnapp, 'L'idée de race et l'archéologie', *Ethnologie française*, no. 2, 1988, pp. 182–7.

13. Including thinkers on the Left, whether socialist, anarchist (Proudhon) or communist, as can be seen from Marx's famous and highly controversial article of 1843 entitled 'On the Jewish Question' (*Early Writings*, Penguin Books in association with New Left Review, Harmondsworth, 1975, pp. 211–41).

14. See Taguieff, *La Force du préjugé*, p. 395.

15. Gabriel Tarde, *Les Lois de l'imitation. Étude sociologique*, Slatkine, Geneva, 1979 (first published in 1895).

16. Claude Lévi-Strauss, *The View from Afar*, trans. J. Neugroschel and P. Hoss, Basic Books, New York, 1985, pp. 14–15.

17. Ludwig Gumplowicz, *La Lutte des races*, Guillaumin, Paris, 1893 (first published in 1883).

18. Quoted by Yves Chevalier, *L'Antisémitisme*, Éditions du Cerf, Paris, 1988, p. 48. On the theme of race in Durkheim, however, see also the chapter 'Race and Society: Primitive and Modern', in Steve Fenton, *Durkheim and Modern Sociology*, Cambridge University Press, Cambridge, 1984.

19. Alexis de Tocqueville, *Democracy in America*, vol. 1, eds J.P. Mayer and Max Lerner, trans. George Lawrence, Collins Fontana, London, 1968 (French original first published in 1835–40), p. 448.

20. Ibid., pp. 450–1.

21. Ibid., p. 443.

22. Several illustrations of this clear and firm position on Max Weber's part are to be found in Freddy Raphaël's *Judaïsme et capitalisme. Essai sur la controverse entre Max Weber et Werner Sombart*, PUF, Paris, 1982. See also Colette Guillaumin and Léon Poliakov, 'Max Weber et les théories bio-raciales du XXᵉ siècle', *Cahiers internationaux de sociologie*, no. 56, 1974, pp. 115–26.

23. Max Weber, *Economy and Society*, vol. 1, trans. Ephraim Fischoff et al., University of California Press, Berkeley/Los Angeles/London, 1978, p. 391.

24. Ibid., p. 385.

25. Ibid., p. 386.

26. John Gabriel and Gideon Ben-Tovim, 'The Conceptualisation of Race Relations in Sociological Theory', *Ethnic and Racial Studies*, vol. II, no. 2, April 1979, pp. 190–212.

27. Cf. Colette Guillaumin, who saw clearly, where the human and natural sciences were concerned, that 'Alexis de Tocqueville never confused the two fields. Max Weber fought a moving struggle against the conflation of the two fields' ('Sciences sociales et définition du terme *race*', in P. Guiral and E. Temime (eds), *L'Idée de race dans la pensée politique française*, CNRS, Paris, 1977).

28. Henry Hughes, *Treatise on Sociology, Theoretical and Practical*, Philadelphia, 1854; George Fitzhugh, *Sociology for the South: Or the Failure of the Society*, Richmond, 1854. For the whole of this paragraph, I have drawn on E. Franklin Frazier, 'Sociological Theory and Race Relations', *American Sociological Review*, vol. 12, no. 3, 1947, pp. 265–71 and E.B. Reuter, 'Racial Theory', *The American Journal of Sociology*, vol. L, no. 6, May 1945, pp. 452–61.

29. Reuter, 'Racial Theory', p. 453.

30. Grove S. Dow, *Society and Its Problems*, New York, 1920.

31. See, for example, the important polemic aroused by Carl Brigham's work, *A Study of American Intelligence* (Princeton University Press, Princeton, 1923), which reports the results of psychological tests taken by soldiers in the American army and suggests a racial explanation of the differences observed, particularly where the lower intelligence of new immigrants is concerned. See also M.R. Neifeld, 'The Race Hypothesis', *The American Journal of Sociology*, vol. XXXII, no. 3, 1926, pp. 423–32.

32. See, for example, together with the articles by Frazier and Reuter cited above, William Julius Wilson, *The Declining Significance of Race*, University of Chicago Press, Chicago, 1978; Thomas Pettigrew (ed.), *The Sociology of Race Relations. Reflection and Reform*, Free Press, New York, 1980 (though the texts published in this work are not really illustrative of this idea in spite of its being very explicitly presented); R. Fred Wacker, *Ethnicity, Pluralism*

and Race. Race Relations Theory in America before Myrdal, Greenwood Press, New York, 1983, who writes, among other things, of a 'racialist' period up to 1920.

33. Madison Grant, *The Passing of a Great Race*, Scribner's, New York, 1916; Lothrop Stoddard, *The Rising Tide of Colour against White World Supremacy*, Scribner's, New York, 1920.

34. Lester F. Ward, *Pure Sociology*, Macmillan, New York, 1921; William G. Sumner, *Folkways*, Ginn, Lexington, 1906; Charles H. Cooley, 'Genius, Fame and Comparisons of Races', *The Annals of the American Academy of Political and Social Science*, vol. IX, May 1897, pp. 1–42, and *Social Organization*, Shocken Books, New York, 1962 (first published in 1932).

Chapter 2

1. The article which really launched this debate was Horace Kallen's 'Democracy versus the Melting Pot', published for the first time in 1915 and reprinted in *Culture and Democracy in the United States*, Boni and Liveright, New York, 1924. On the debate on the American 'non-melting pot', see Stephen Steinberg, *The Ethnic Myth. Race, Ethnicity and Class in America*, Beacon Press, Boston, 1989 (first published in 1981).

2. W.E.B. Du Bois, *The Philadelphia Negro. A Social Study*, University of Pennsylvania Press, Philadelphia, 1899.

3. On the importance of Franz Boas, see especially Gunnar Myrdal, *An American Dilemma. The Negro Problem and Modern Democracy*, Harper and Row, New York, 1944, 2 vols; Gilbert Freyre, *Maîtres et esclaves*, Gallimard, Paris, 1974 (first published in 1933). The quotation from Boas is taken from Maurice Olender, 'La chasse aux évidences', in *Le Racisme. Mythes et sciences*, Complexe, Brussels, 1981, p. 228. Ambiguous formulations on race have been pointed out in the first edition of Franz Boas's *The Mind of Primitive Man* (Macmillan, New York, 1911), but these had disappeared from the 1938 edition).

4. Lester F. Ward, *Pure Sociology*, New York, 1921.

5. Charles H. Cooley, 'Genius, Fame and Comparison of Races'. This article is reprinted in *Sociological Theory and Social Research: Being Selected Papers of Charles Horton Cooley*, Henry Holt, New York, 1930, pp. 121–59.

6. On racial problems, as they appear in the work of Park, see in particular the chapter entitled 'Racial Conflicts' in Robert E. Park and Ernest W. Burgess (eds), *Introduction to the Science of Sociology*, Greenwood Press, New York, 1924, pp. 619–34, and the many articles gathered together after his death and published as *Race and Culture, Collected Papers*, vol. I, Free Press, Glencoe, IL, 1950. On the variations to be found in his work, see E. Franklin Frazier, 'Sociological Theory and Race Relations', *American Sociological Review*, vol. 12, no. 3, 1947, pp. 269–70.

7. Robert E. Park, *Race and Culture*, p. 116.

8. Bertram W. Doyle, *The Etiquette of Race Relations in the South*, Chicago University Press, Chicago, 1922; cf. Park, *Race and Culture*, especially p. 184.

9. Park, *Race and Culture*, p. 227.

10. See Chicago Commission on Race Relations, *The Negro in Chicago*, University of Chicago Press, Chicago, 1922. For an analysis of Robert E. Park's commitment and role, see Martin Bulmer, 'Charles S. Johnson, Robert E. Park and the Research Methods of the Chicago Commission on Race Relations, 1919–1922. An Early Experiment in Applied Social Research', *Ethnic and Racial Studies*, vol. IV, no. 3, July 1981, pp. 289–306.

11. Park, *Race and Culture*, p. 81.

12. Ibid., p. 81. This idea was later to be greatly developed by other writers, notably Herbert Blumer. See, for example, that author's 'Race Prejudice as a Sense of Group Position', *Pacific Sociological Review*, no. 1, 1958, pp. 3–7.

13. Ladner quotes some passages from the *Introduction to the Science of Sociology* (pp. 138–9) in which Park and Burgess describe the 'temperament' of the negro, his distinctive, biologically transmitted characteristics, his disposition towards expressiveness

rather than enterprise and action, etc. (Joyce A. Ladner [ed.], *The Death of White Sociology*, Vintage Books, New York, 1973, pp. xxi–xxii.

14. Everett C. Hughes and Helen MacGill Hughes, *Where Peoples Meet. Racial and Ethnic Frontiers*, Greenwood Press, Westport, CT, 1981 (first published in 1952), p. 19.

15. Ibid., p. 51.

16. Robert E. Park, 'Human Migration and the Marginal Man', *The American Journal of Sociology*, vol. XXXIII, no. 6, May 1928, p. 890.

17. Robert E. Park, 'The Basis of Race Prejudice', *The Annals of the American Academy of Political and Social Sciences*, vol. CXXXX ('The American Negro'), November 1928, p. 13 (quoted by Frazier, 'Sociological Theory and Race Relations', p. 169, and by Myrdal, *An American Dilemma*, p. 662).

18. On the criticism of the notion of race as it appears in 'race relations' theory, see Robert Miles, 'Beyond the Race Concept. The Reproduction of Racism in England', in M. de Lepervanche and G. Bottomley (eds), *The Cultural Construction of Race*, Sydney Association for Studies in Society and Culture, Sydney, 1988, pp. 7–31.

19. Park, 'The Basis of Race Prejudice', p. 20.

20. See W. Lloyd Warner, 'American Caste and Class', *The American Journal of Sociology*, vol. XLII, no. 2, Sept. 1936, pp. 234–7 (fig. is on p. 235); W. Lloyd Warner, 'Introduction' to Allison Davis, Burleigh B. and Mary R. Gardner, *Deep South. A Social Anthropological Study of Caste and Class*, University of Chicago Press, Chicago, 1941, p. 10.

21. W.E.B. Du Bois, *Dusk of Dawn. An Essay towards an Autobiography of a Race Concept*, Harcourt, Brace and Co., New York, 1940, p. 183; Myrdal, *An American Dilemma*, pp. 691–3; Oliver Cox, 'The Modern Caste School of Race Relations', *Social Forces*, no. 21, December 1942, pp. 218–26.

22. See Michael Banton, *Racial Theories*, Cambridge University Press, Cambridge, 1987, p. 100.

23. See, in particular, William Julius Wilson, *The Declining Significance of Race*. University of Chicago Press, Chicago, 1978.

24. Davis et al., *Deep South*; John Dollard, *Caste and Class in a Southern Town*, University of Wisconsin Press, Madison, 1988 (first published in 1937).

Chapter 3

1. John Dollard, *Caste and Class in a Southern Town*, University of Wisconsin Press, Madison, 1988, p. 441.

2. Ibid, p. x. In his preface to the 1957 edition, Dollard pays tribute to Edward Sapir and his Yale seminar on the impact of culture on personality.

3. Eugene L. Horowitz, 'The Development of Attitudes toward the Negro', *Arch. Psychol.*, no. 194, January 1936, pp. 34–5 (quoted by Dollard, *Caste and Class in a Southern Town*, p. 445).

4. Dollard, *Caste and Class in a Southern Town*, p. 445.

5. Gunnar Myrdal, *An American Dilemma. The Negro Problem and Modern Democracy*, Harper and Row, New York, 1944, 2 vols.

6. Ibid., vol. 1, p. xliii.

7. Ibid., vol. 1, p. xlvii.

8. Ibid., vol. 1, p. 41.

9. Ralph Ellison, *Invisible Man*, Random House, New York, 1952.

10. Myrdal, *An American Dilemma*, vol. 1, p. 68.

11. See Pierre-André Taguieff, *La Force du préjugé. Essai sur le racisme et ses doubles*, La Découverte, Paris, 1988, pp. 348–54.

12. Myrdal, *An American Dilemma*, vol. 1, chapter 45, pp. 997–1024.

13. See Michael Banton, *The Idea of Race*, Tavistock, London, 1977, p. 12.

14. See, in particular, by these authors: Hans Eysenck, *The Psychology of Politics*, Routledge and Kegan Paul, London, 1954; Gordon W. Allport, *The Nature of Prejudice*, Addison-Wesley, Reading, MA, 1987 (first published in 1954); Otto Klineberg, 'Race et

psychologie', *Le Racisme devant la science*, UNESCO-Gallimard, Paris, 1960, and *Psychologie sociale* (2 vols), PUF, Paris, 1957 and 1959.

15. Bruno Bettelheim and Morris Janowitz, *Social Change and Prejudice*, Free Press, New York, 1964; Leo Lowenthal and Norbert Guterman, *Prophets of Deceit. A Study of the Technics of the American Agitator*, Harper and Brothers, New York, 1949.

16. Theodor W. Adorno, Else Frenkel-Brunswik, Daniel J. Levinson, R. Nevitt Sanford, in collaboration with Betty Aron, Maria Hertz Levinson and William Morrow, *The Authoritarian Personality*, Harper and Brothers, New York, 1950.

17. Ibid., p. 6.

18. Milton Rokeach, *The Open and Closed Mind*, Basic Books, New York, 1960.

19. Jean-Paul Sartre, *Anti-Semite and Jew*, trans. George J. Becker, Shocken Books, New York, 1965.

20. Adorno et al., *The Authoritarian Personality*, p. 5.

21. Jean-Paul Sartre, *Anti-Semite and Jew*, p. 143.

22. Allport, *The Nature of Prejudice*, p. 9.

23. Albert Jacquard and J.-B. Pontalis, 'Entretien: une tête qui ne convient pas', *Le Genre humain*, no. 11, 1984–5, pp. 15–28.

24. Julia Kristeva, *Strangers to Ourselves*, trans. Leon S. Roudiez, Columbia University Press, New York, 1991, p. 191.

25. See, for example, François Jacob: 'What biology can, in the end, assert is that:
– the concept of race has lost all operative value and can only rigidify our vision of what is a ceaselessly shifting reality,
– the mechanism of transmission of life is such that each individual is unique, that individuals cannot be ranked hierarchically, that the only treasure here is a collective one: it is made up of diversity. All the rest is ideology' ('Biologie – racisme – hiérarchie', in Maurice Olender (ed.), *Le Racisme. Mythes et sciences*, Complexe, Brussels, 1981, p. 109).

26. We might have provided a fourth dimension of this fragmentation by adding propositions which impute racism not to the racializing group, but to the racialized one. This point of view, itself very close to the most elementary racist discourse, may, when argued by a member of a racialized group, attest to a certain alienation. It has never, in fact, had much force in the social sciences, and even a man like Bernard Lazare, who put this argument in *L'Antisémitisme, son histoire et ses causes* (Jean Crès, Paris, 1894), explaining the origin of anti-semitism by the desire of the Jews to remain separate – revised this idea in his later writings. But, as we have already pointed out, it is also true that the transmission of Jewishness, according to Jewish law, is itself related to a biological principle.

Chapter 4

1. Hannah Arendt, *The Origins of Totalitarianism*, André Deutsch, London, 1968, p. 159.

2. Ibid.

3. Ibid., p. 172.

4. Ibid.

5. Ibid., p. 170.

6. Ibid., pp. 182–3.

7. Ibid., p. 180.

8. See, for example, Pierre Ayçoberry, *The Nazi Question. An Essay on the Interpretation of National-Socialism (1922–1975)*, trans. Robert Hurley, Routledge and Kegan Paul, London, 1981, who speaks of Arendt's book creating 'a false impression' and refers to it as an 'accumulation of brilliant paradoxes and contradictory assertions' (p. 130).

9. Louis Dumont, *Essais sur l'individualisme*, Éditions du Seuil, Paris, 1987, p. 19. [*Translator's note*: The passage in question is from the Introduction to the French edition, and is not in the English translation.]

10. Louis Dumont, *Homo aequalis*, Gallimard, Paris, 1977.

11. *Essais sur l'individualisme*, p. 28.

12. Louis Dumont, *Essays on Individualism*, University of Chicago Press, Chicago and London, 1986, pp. 150, 153, 158.

13. Ibid., p. 176.

14. Ibid., p. 178.

15. See Tzvetan Todorov, *Nous et les Autres*, Éditions du Seuil, Paris, 1989, p. 435: 'it is precisely as though the victory of the individualistic ideology, on which modern democracies are based, were accompanied by the repression of holistic values, which would not accept being treated in this way and would resurface in those more or less monstrous forms that are nationalism, racism or the totalitarian utopia.'

16. See Alain Renaut, *L'Ère de l'individu*, Gallimard, Paris, 1989, particularly chapter II of part I, entitled 'Louis Dumont, le triomphe de l'individu', in which he criticizes Dumont for his ignorance of the fact that modernity bears within it an internal conflict; that it does not only – or necessarily – represent the triumph of the individual, the market or narcissism, but is also the site of the constitution of the subject.

17. See Christian Delacampagne, *L'Invention du racisme*, Fayard, Paris, 1983, p. 58: 'Racism is older than the Enlightenment. It is older than egalitarian society. One cannot even say that it is linked to a type of social organization.' Delacampagne is not always as radical as these lines suggest: when he examines the 'racism of the Middle Ages or Antiquity', it is to look for the mark or prefiguring of socio-cultural principles which will be those of the modern world.

18. Colette Guillaumin, *L'Idéologie raciste. Genèse et langage actuel*, Mouton, The Hague, 1972, p. 92.

19. Léon Poliakov, *The History of Anti-Semitism* (vols 1–3), Routledge and Kegan Paul, London, 1974–5 (vol. 4, Oxford University Press, Oxford, 1985).

20. Georges Élias Sarfati, 'Entretien avec Léon Poliakov', in *L'Envers du destin*, Calmann-Lévy, Paris, 1989, p. 87.

21. See, especially, Maxime Rodinson, 'Critiques sur la démarche poliakovienne', in Maurice Olender (ed.), *Le Racisme. Mythes et sciences*, Complexe, Brussels, 1981, p. 318.

22. In Sarfati, *L'Envers du destin*, p. 124.

23. Anthony D. Smith, *The Ethnic Origins of Nations*, Oxford, 1987.

24. See Léon Poliakov, *The Aryan Myth. A History of Racist and Nationalist Ideas in Europe*, trans. Edmund Howard, Basic Books, New York, 1971.

25. In Sarfati, *L'Envers du destin*, pp. 130–1.

26. Léon Poliakov, *La Causalité diabolique. Essai sur l'origine des persécutions*, Calmann-Lévy, Paris, 1980.

27. *The History of Anti-Semitism*, vol. 4: *Suicidal Europe, 1870–1933*, trans. George Klin, Oxford University Press, Oxford, 1985, p. 32.

28. Norman Cohn, *Warrant for Genocide. The Myth of the Jewish World Conspiracy and the Protocols of the Elders of Zion*, Eyre and Spottiswoode, London, 1967.

29. Jacob Katz, *From Prejudice to Destruction. Anti-Semitism 1700–1933*, Harvard University Press, Cambridge, MA, 1980.

30. Pierre Birnbaum, *Un mythe politique: la République juive*, Fayard, Paris, 1988.

Conclusion

1. Pierre van den Berghe, *Race and Racism. A Comparative Perspective*, 2nd edn, Wiley, New York, 1978, p. xv. On these problems of – social or biological – definition of race and what may be gained by resorting to the notion of ethnic group, cf. J. Milton Yinger, 'Intersecting Strands in the Theorisation of Race and Ethnic Relations', in John Rex and David Mason (eds), *Theories of Race and Ethnic Relations*, Cambridge University Press, Cambridge, 1986, pp. 20–41.

2. Yves Chevalier, *L'Antisémitisme*, Éditions du Cerf, Paris, 1988. See, in particular, the overall conclusion to the work: 'the model of the scapegoat allows us, it seems to me, to integrate these partial theories into a more complex whole' (p. 385).

Part Two

Introduction

1. John Rex, *Colonialism and the City*, Oxford University Press, London, 1973.
2. Richard A. Schermerhorn, *Comparative Ethnic Relations. A Framework for Theory and Research*, University of Chicago Press, Chicago, 1978 (first published in 1970).
3. See especially Nonna Mayer, 'Ethnocentrisme, racisme et intolérance', in CEVIFOP, *L'Électeur français en question*, FNSP, Paris, 1990, pp. 17–43.
4. See, for example, Pierre-André Taguieff, *La Force du préjugé. Essai sur le racisme et ses doubles*, La Découverte, Paris, 1988, who mentions this way of dividing up the material several times; George M. Frederickson, 'Toward a Social Interpretation of the Development of American Racism', in N. Higgins, M. Kilson and D. Fox (eds), *Key Issues in the Afro-American Experience*, Harcourt Brace Jovanovitch, New York, 1971; or Donald L. Noel (ed.), *The Origins of American Slavery and Racism*, Charles E. Merrill, Columbus, 1972.

Chapter 5

1. Michael Pollak, 'Utopie et échec d'une science raciale', in A. Bégin and J. Freund (eds), *Racismes, Antiracismes*, Klincksieck, Paris, 1986, p. 197.
2. Benno Müller-Hill, *Murderous Science. Elimination by Scientific Selection of Jews, Gypsies, and Others, Germany 1933–45*, trans. George R. Fraser, Oxford University Press, Oxford/New York/Tokyo, 1988, p. 42.
3. Richard T. LaPiere, 'Attitudes versus Actions', *Social Forces*, 13, 1934, pp. 230–7.
4. Gordon W. Allport, *The Nature of Prejudice*, Addison-Wesley, Reading, MA, 1987, p. 57.
5. Colette Guillaumin, *L'Idéologie raciste. Genèse et langage actuel*, Mouton, The Hague, 1972, p. 8.
6. Ibid., p. 47.
7. Ibid., p. 61.
8. Martin Barker, *The New Racism*, Junction Books, London, 1981.
9. For a (very critical) presentation of the 'new racism' concept, see Robert Miles, *Racism*, Routledge, London, 1989, pp. 62–6.
10. Pierre-André Taguieff, *La Force du préjugé. Essai sur le racisme et ses doubles*, La Découverte, Paris, 1988, p. 14.
11. Ibid., pp. 162–76. Among other writers who have also noted the existence of these two logics, see Alain de Benoist, 'Racisme: remarques autour d'une définition', in Bégin and Freund (eds), *Racismes, Antiracismes*, pp. 203–51.
12. See, for example, Alain Touraine, *The Voice and the Eye. An Analysis of Social Movements*, trans. Alan Duff, Cambridge University Press/Éditions de la maison des sciences de l'homme, Cambridge etc./Paris, 1981.

Chapter 6

1. Pierre-André Taguieff, *La Force du préjugé. Essai sur le racisme et ses doubles*, La Découverte, Paris, 1988, see, especially, chapter VI, pp. 240–70.
2. Theodor W. Adorno, Else Frenkel-Brunswik, Daniel J. Levinson, R. Nevitt Sanford, in collaboration with Betty Aron, Maria Hertz Levinson and William Morrow, Harper and Brothers, New York, 1950, *The Authoritarian Personality*; Erich Fromm, (*Fear of Freedom*, Routledge and Kegan Paul, London, 1960), 'in whose view, the prejudiced individual is incapable of having authentic personal relations with others and forms bonds with the outside world by constructing fantasized figures of good (heroes) and evil (ethnic groups).' Milton Rokeach, *The Open and Closed Mind*, Basic Books, New York, 1960.
3. Cited by Michael Billig, 'Racisme, préjugés et discrimination', in Serge Moscovici (ed.), *Psychologie sociale*, PUF, Paris, pp. 449–72. We may note that, in 'New Black–White

136   NOTES

Patterns: How Best to Conceptualize Them' (*Annual Review of Sociology*, no. 11, 1985, pp. 329–46), Thomas Pettigrew calls for a balance to be struck, in the research into racial attitudes, between social and personality factors.

4. Richard A. Schermerhorn, *Comparative Ethnic Relations. A Framework for Theory and Research*, University of Chicago Press, Chicago, 1978, p. 6.

5. On the relationship between ethnocentrism and racism, see Vittorio Lanternari, 'Ethnocentrism and Ideology', *Ethnic and Racial Studies*, vol. 3, no. 1, January 1980, pp. 52–66.

6. See, for example, Christian Delacampagne (*L'Invention du racisme*, Fayard, Paris, 1983), who points out in Jean-Paul Sartre's *Anti-Semite and Jew* several formulations which may be read, anachronistically, as incredibly racist.

7. Gérard Lemaine and James S. Jackson, 'Éditorial', *Revue internationale de psychologie sociale*, no. 3, 1989, p. 271. See also J.M. Jones (*Prejudice and Racism*, Addison-Wesley, Reading, MA, 1972), who finds unacceptable the idea that prejudice should be seen as a departure from egalitarian norms or as something initially individual.

8. See Gordon W. Allport, *The Nature of Prejudice*, Addison-Wesley, Reading, MA, 1987, chapter 13, 'Theories of Prejudice', pp. 206–18.

9. Otto Klineberg, *Psychologie sociale*, PUF, Paris, 1959, vol. II, chapter IX.

10. See, in particular, George M. Fredrickson, 'Toward a Social Interpretation of the Development of American Racism', in N. Higgins, M. Kilson and D. Fox (eds), *Key Issues in the Afro-American Experience*, Harcourt Brace Jovanovitch, New York, 1971.

11. Teun A. Van Dijk, *Communicating Racism. Ethnic Prejudice in Thought and Talk*, Sage, Newbury Park, 1987.

12. Michael Hechter, 'Rational Choice Theory and the Study of Race and Ethnic Relations', in John Rex and David Mason (eds), *Theories of Race and Ethnic Relations*, Cambridge University Press, Cambridge, 1986, pp. 264–79; Michael Banton, *Racial Theories*, Cambridge University Press, Cambridge, 1987, pp. 121–35, or 'Two Theories of Racial Discrimination in Housing', *Ethnic and Racial Studies*, vol. 2, no. 4, October 1979, pp. 416–27.

13. George Eaton Simpson and J. Milton Yinger, *Racial and Cultural Minorities*, Plenum, London/NY, 1985, p. 158.

14. Edgar Morin, *Rumour in Orléans*, trans. Peter Green, Anthony Blond, London, 1971.

15. Ibid., p. 56.

16. Ibid., p. 74.

17. Cornelius Castoriadis, Claude Lefort and Edgar Morin, *Mai 1968: la brèche*, Fayard, Paris, 1968.

18. See Eugene L. Hartley, *Problems in Prejudice*, King's Crown Press, New York, 1946 (quoted by Simpson and Yinger, *Racial and Cultural Minorities*, p. 95).

19. Cf. Thomas Pettigrew, 'The Nature of Modern Racism in the United States', *Revue internationale de psychologie sociale*, pp. 293–302.

20. On symbolic racism, see especially Donald R. Kinder and David O. Sears, 'Prejudice and Politics: Symbolic Racism Threats to the Good Life', *Journal of Personality and Social Psychology*, vol. 40, no. 3, 1981, pp. 414–31; David O. Sears, 'Symbolic Racism', in Phyllis A. Katz and Dalmas A. Taylor (eds), *Eliminating Racism*, Plenum Press, New York, 1988, pp. 53–84, and, in the same work: Lawrence Bobo, 'Group Conflict, Prejudice and Paradox of Contemporary Racial Attitudes', pp. 85–114.

21. On the contemporary phenomenon of the decline of the American middle classes, see, for example, Katherine S. Newman, *Falling from Grace. The Experience of Downward Mobility in the American Middle Class*, Vintage Books, New York, 1989.

22. Morin, *Rumour in Orléans*, pp. 42–3.

Chapter 7

1. See C. Van Woodward, *Origins of the New South 1877–1913*, Louisiana State University Press, Baton Rouge, 1951.

2. See Michel Wieviorka, 'La crise du modèle français d'intégration', *Regards sur l'actualité*, no. 161, May 1990, pp. 3–15.

3. See Thomas Sowell, *Race and Economics*, David McKay Co., New York, 1975; *Market and Minorities*, Basic Books, New York, 1981. For analysis of Sowell's thinking, see Pierre-André Taguieff, *La Force du préjugé. Essai sur le racisme et ses doubles*, La Découverte, Paris, 1988, pp. 260–6.

4. Gary S. Becker, *The Economics of Discrimination*, University of Chicago Press, Chicago, 1957.

5. Judith Shapiro, 'What is New in the Economics of Racial Discrimination?', *Ethnic and Racial Studies*, vol. 6, no. 1, January 1983, pp. 111–18.

6. According to the 'zonal hypothesis', every city tends to expand radially from its business centre. This is initially encircled by a transitional area, invaded by business and light manufacture, which is inhabited by the workers in industries who have escaped from the area of deterioration but wish to live within easy access of their work; then come a bourgeois, residential area, a suburban area and, lastly, satellite cities. According to this hypothesis, every city expands by extending into the neighbouring zone, in ways not dissimilar, says Burgess, to the processes studied in plant ecology. See Ernest W. Burgess, 'The Growth of the City. An Introduction to a Research Project', in Robert E. Park, Ernest W. Burgess and Roderick D. McKenzie, *The City*, University of Chicago Press, Chicago/London, 1967 (first published in 1925), pp. 47–62.

7. Ibid., p. 54.

8. Ibid., p. 56.

9. Louis Wirth, *The Ghetto*, University of Chicago Press, Chicago, 3rd impression, 1946 (first published in 1928), p. 18.

10. Robert E. Park, 'The City. Suggestions for the Investigation of Human Behaviour in the Urban Environment', in Park et al., *The City*, pp. 40–1.

11. Georg Simmel, 'The Stranger', in Kurt H. Wolff (ed.), *The Sociology of Georg Simmel*, Free Press, Glencoe, IL, 1950, pp. 402–8 (first published in 1908); Robert E. Park, 'Human Migration and the Marginal Man', *The American Journal of Sociology*, vol. XXXIII, no. 6, May 1928, pp. 881–93.

12. Emory S. Bogardus, 'A Race Relations Cycle', *The American Journal of Sociology*, vol. XXXV, no. 4, January 1930, p. 613. For other authors developing schemata of this kind, see Brewton Barry, *Race and Ethnic Relations*, Riverside Press, Boston, 1958.

13. See René Duchac, *La Sociologie des migrations aux États-Unis*, Mouton, Paris, 1974, p. 120.

14. Otis D. and Beverley Duncan, *The Negro Population of Chicago. A Study of Residential Succession*, 2nd edn, University of Chicago Press, Chicago, 1965.

15. Duchac, *La sociologie des migrations aux États-Unis*.

16. Karl E. Teuber, 'Negro Residential Segregation. Trends and Measurement', *Social Problems*, vol. XII, no. I, summer 1964, pp. 42–50; Stanley Lieberson, *Ethnic Patterns in American Cities*, Free Press of Glencoe, New York, 1963.

17. St Clair Drake and Horace R. Cayton, *Black Metropolis. A Study of Negro Life in a Northern City*, Harper and Row, New York, 1962, 2 vols (first published in 1945).

18. René Duchac (*La Sociologie des migrations aux États-Unis*, pp. 392–3) quotes several convergent pieces of work which show that 'for equal quality, blacks always pay more', and if, for example, whites who are in a hurry to leave in a period of black 'invasion' often sell their properties at a loss, others – particularly estate agents – make money from this situation and keep the market at a more or less equal level.

19. William J. Wilson, *The Declining Significance of Race*, University of Chicago Press, Chicago, 1978; see also his *The Truly Disadvantaged. The Inner City, the Underclass and Public Policy*, University of Chicago Press, Chicago, 1987.

20. Loïc Wacquant and William J. Wilson, 'The Cost of Racial and Class Exclusion in the Inner City', *The Annals of the American Academy of Political and Social Science*, January 1989, pp. 8–25.

21. See, in particular, the work by Peter Doeringer and Michael J. Piore, 'Unemployment and the Dual Labor Market', *The Public Interest*, no. 38, winter 1975, pp. 67–79; 'Equal Employment Opportunity in Boston', *Industrial Relations*, no. 9, May 1970, pp. 324–9; Robert T. Averitt, *The Dual Economy*, Norton, New York, 1968; James O'Connor, *The Fiscal Crisis of the State*, St Martin's Press, New York, 1973; and, more recently, Michael Piore and Charles F. Sabel, *The Second Industrial Divide. Possibilities for Prosperity*, Basic Books, New York, 1984.

22. E. Franklin Frazier, *Black Bourgeoisie*, The Free Press, New York, 1957.

23. Kenneth B. Clark, 'The Role of Race', *The New York Times Magazine*, 5 October 1980.

24. See Alphonso Pinkney (*The Myth of Black Progress*, Cambridge University Press, Cambridge, 1984), who cites the highly polemical criticisms of the American Association of Black Sociologists, which he also personally endorses, and who regards the idea of black progress as a myth.

25. To make this point clearer, let us add that historians have shown that in the southern states of the USA the traditional plantation- and slavery-based economy did not generate spatial segregation. See E. Franklin Frazier (*Race and Culture Contrasts in the Modern World*, Alfred A. Knopf, New York, 1957), who points out that, 'Contrary to popular notions, the Negro was not segregated in the older cities of the South. They were brought to these cities by their white owners before the Civil War and it became customary for Negroes and whites to live in the same residential areas. It was in the border cities, where the location of Negroes was determined neither by economic factors nor by historical traditions and custom, that the residential segregation of Negroes became a matter for legislation' (p. 282). For the effects which are still felt today of the old southern model, see Lee F. Schnore and Philip C. Evenson, 'Segregation in Southern Cities', *The American Journal of Sociology*, vol. LXXII, no. 1, July 1966, pp. 58–67.

26. Michael Banton, 'Two Theories of Racial Discrimination in Housing', *Ethnic and Racial Studies*, vol. 2, no. 4, October 1979, pp. 416–27. The idea of a free and open market may itself be complexified, for example, with the aid of the alternative idea of a dualization of the housing market. See Linda Brewster Stearns and John R. Logan, 'The Racial Structuring of the Housing Market and Segregation in Suburban Areas', *Social Forces*, vol. 65, no. 1, September 1986, pp. 28-42. See also the work of John Rex, especially John Rex and Robert Moore, *Race Community and Conflict. A Study of Sparkbrook*, Oxford University Press, London, 1967; John Rex, *Race and Ethnicity*, Open University Press, Milton Keynes, 1986.

27. From among a huge literature on this subject, see Pierre L. van den Berghe, *South Africa. A Study in Conflict*, University of California Press, Berkeley; Leonard Thompson and A. Prior, *South African Politics*, Yale University Press, New Haven, 1982; J. Lelyveld, *Move Your Shadow. South Africa, Black and White*, Times Books, New York, 1985; Leonard Thompson, *The Political Mythology of Apartheid*, Yale University Press, New Haven, 1985.

28. See Benjamin B. Ringer and Elinor R. Lawless, *Race, Ethnicity and Society*, Routledge, New York, 1989, pp. 113–18.

29. See, for example, Robert L. Crain ('School Integration and Occupational Achievement of Negroes', in Thomas Pettigrew (ed.), *Racial Discrimination in the United States*, Harper and Row, New York, 1975, pp. 206–24), who shows that in the United States in the 1960s blacks educated in 'integrated' schools have greater chances of occupying jobs traditionally reserved for whites: they benefit from networks of friendship between whites and blacks which go on after school and belong to broad information networks which are crucial in finding employment.

30. See, for example, the list to which Gordon W. Allport refers in *The Nature of Prejudice*, Addison-Wesley, Reading, MA, 1987, p. 52.

31. Among what is, here again, a great wealth of literature on this subject, see, for an interesting summary of the UK situation, Richard Jenkins, *Racism and Recruitment*, Cambridge University Press, Cambridge, 1986.

32. See Marvin E. Wolfgang and Bernard Cohen ('Crime and Race', in Pettigrew (ed.), *Racial Discrimination in the United States*, pp. 284–302), who cite some edifying figures, showing that, statistically, a black man pays more dearly for his crime than a white man: for

example, between 1940 and 1984 in Florida, blacks who raped white women were condemned to death in 54 per cent of cases whereas the rate for whites raping black women was 0 per cent.

33. Cf. George Lowe and Eugene Hodges, 'Race and the Treatment of Alcoholism in a Southern State', *Social Problems*, no. 20, 1972, pp. 240–52.

34. Stokely Carmichael and Charles Hamilton, *Black Power*, Vintage Books, New York, 1967.

35. See Robert Blauner, *Racial Oppression in America*, Harper and Row, New York, 1972, pp. 9–10.

36. Whitney Young, *To Be Equal*, McGraw-Hill, New York, 1964, p. 18 (quoted by Robert Friedman, 'Institutional Racism. How to Discriminate without Really Trying', in Pettigrew (ed.), *Racial Discrimination in the United States*, pp. 384–407).

37. Friedman, 'Institutional Racism', p. 387.

38. Ibid., p. 422.

39. For a presentation of this orientation, as applied to the question of racism, particularly in the United Kingdom, see John Solomos, *Race and Racism in Contemporary Britain*, Macmillan, London, 1989, pp. 16–21.

40. See Ambalavaner Sivanandan, 'Race, Class and Power. An Outline for Study', *Race*, vol. 14, no. 4, 1973, pp. 383–91; 'RAT and the Degradation of the Black Struggle', *Race and Class*, vol. 26, no. 4, 1985, pp. 1–34. For a critique of Sivanandan's terminological variations, see Robert Miles, *Racism*, Routledge, London, 1989, pp. 53–4.

41. Robert Merton, 'Discrimination and the American Creed', in R. MacIver (ed.), *Discrimination and National Welfare*, Harper and Row, New York, 1949.

42. David T. Wellman, *Portraits of White Racism*, Cambridge University Press, Cambridge, 1977.

43. See Didier Lapeyronnie and Marcin Frybes, *L'Intégration des minorités immigrées. Étude comparative France–Grande-Bretagne*, ADRI-BIT, Paris, 1990.

Chapter 8

1. Serge Moscovici, 'Le ressentiment', *Le Genre humain*, no. 11, autumn–winter, 1984–5, p. 181.

2. Gordon W. Allport, *The Nature of Prejudice*, Addison-Wesley, Reading, MA, 1987, pp. 57–8.

3. Michel Wieviorka, *Sociétés et terrorisme*, Fayard, Paris, 1988. part V, chapter II, 'Le terrorisme palestinien', pp. 381–408.

4. Ibid., 'Annexe théorique', pp. 460–91; cf. also James B. Rule, *Theories of Civil Violence*, University of California Press, Berkeley, 1988.

5. Serge Moscovici, *The Age of the Crowd: a historical treatise on mass psychology*, trans. J.C. Whitehouse, Cambridge University Press/Éditions de la Maison des Sciences de l'Homme, Cambridge, 1985, p. 96.

6. Cf. William Kornhauser, *The Politics of Mass Society*, Free Press of Glencoe, Glencoe, IL, 1959.

7. Ted Robert Gurr, 'Urban Disorder. Perspectives from the Comparative Study of Civil Strife', in Allen D. Grimshaw (ed.), *Racial Violence in the United States*, Aldine Publishing Co., Chicago, 1969, p. 371.

8. Might I refer the reader, here, to the analyses I advanced in the theoretical annex to – and throughout – my work, *Sociétés et terrorisme*.

9. See, in particular, the monumental study by Raoul Hillberg, *La Destruction des Juifs d'Europe*, Fayard, Paris, 1988.

10. Ibid., especially pp. 40–8.

11. Walter Laqueur, *The Terrible Secret. An Investigation into the Suppression of Information about Hitler's 'Final Solution'*, Weidenfeld and Nicholson, London, 1980.

12. Grimshaw (ed.), *Racial Violence in the United States*.

13. Jean-Claude Monet, 'Société multiraciale et comportements policiers'. Paper given at the conference, *Police et société de demain*, 23 November 1988, p. 7.

14. See Michel Wieviorka, *Les Juifs, la Pologne et Solidarnosc*, Denoël, Paris, 1984, pp. 115–18.

15. Simon Doubnov, *Histoire d'un soldat juif, 1880–1915*, Éditions du Cerf, Paris, 1988.

16. A few months before his death, Stalin had accused the Jewish doctors attending him of plotting his murder.

17. Grimshaw (ed.), *Racial Violence in the United States*.

18. See Arthur F. Raper, *The Tragedy of Lynching*, University of North Carolina Press, Chapel Hill, 1933; Hadley Cantril, *The Psychology of Social Movements*, Wiley, New York, 1941; together with Gunnar Myrdal, *An American Dilemma. The Negro Problem and Modern Democracy*, Harper and Row, New York, 1944, 2 vols, and Allport, *The Nature of Prejudice*; see also Jean Stoetzel, *La Psychologie sociale*, Flammarion, Paris, 1963, pp. 230–2.

19. We should point out that there is still lively controversy around the theme of lynching. On the correlation between lynching and the economic situation, see especially Carl Iver Hovland and Robert R. Sears, 'Minor Studies in Aggression. Correlation of Lynchings with Economic Indices', *Journal of Psychology*, no. 9, 1940, pp. 301–10. And, for a critique suggesting the correlation is a statistical artefact, Alexander Mintz, 'A Re-examination of Correlations between Lynchings and Economic Indices', *Journal of Abnormal and Social Psychology*, no. 41, 1946, pp. 154–60. On the argument that there is a link between lynching and the maintenance of political domination by the use of threat, see particularly Hubert Blalock, *Toward a Theory of Minority Group Relations*, Wiley, New York, 1967, and the March 1989 number of *Social Forces* (vol. 67, no. 3), which contains the following articles: Stewart E. Tolnay, E.M. Beck and James L. Massey, 'Black Lynchings. The Power Threat Hypothesis Revisited' (pp. 605–23); John Skelton Reed, 'Comment on Tolnay, Beck and Massey' (pp. 624–5); James C. Creech, Jay Corzine and Lin Huff-Corzine, 'Theory Testing and Lynching. Another Look at the Power Threat Hypothesis' (pp. 626–30); H.M. Blalock, 'Percent Black and Lynchings Revisited' (pp. 631–40).

20. For a very detailed account, see Marc Hillel, *Le Massacre des survivants en Pologne, 1945–1947*, Plon, Paris, 1985.

Part Three

Introduction

1. See Alain Touraine, *The Voice and the Eye. An Analysis of Social Movements*, trans. Alan Duff, Cambridge University Press/Éditions de la maison des sciences de l'homme, Cambridge etc./Paris, 1981.

2. Albert Memmi, *Le Racisme*, Gallimard, Paris, 1982, p. 35.

3. This third part draws on analyses already outlined in my papers 'Mouvements sociaux et racisme' and 'Nature et formation des mouvements communautaires', delivered to the International Congress of Sociology, Madrid, 1990, and CEDEJ and IEDES Conference, Cairo, 1989, respectively.

Chapter 9

1. Pierre Milza, *Français et Italiens à la fin du XIXe siècle*, École française de Rome, Rome, 1981. The anti-Italian violence which came to a head at Aigues-Mortes in 1893 caused eight deaths according to the official figures. For an overall view of this type of violence in France, see Gérard Noiriel, *Le Creuset français*, Éditions du Seuil, Paris, 1986, pp. 257–62. On the Left of the labour movement and anti-semitism, see Michel Winock, *Édouard Drumont, et al., Antisémitisme et Fascisme en France*, Éditions du Seuil, Paris, 1982. On American trade unionism and its relationship with blacks, see, for example, H. Hill, 'The Racial Practices of Organised Labour', in A.M. Ross, H. Hill (eds), *Employment, Race and Poverty*, Harcourt,

Brace and Worth, New York, 1967; S.D. Spero and A.L. Harris, *The Black Worker*, Atheneum, New York, 1974.

2. Hadley Cantril, *The Psychology of Social Movements*, Wiley, New York, 1941; Birgitta Orfali, *L'Adhésion au Front national. De la minorité active au mouvement social*, Kimé, Paris, 1990.

3. See Alain Touraine, *The Self-Production of Society*, trans. Derek Coltman, University of Chicago Press, Chicago, 1977.

4. Abraham Léon, *La Conception matérialiste de la question juive*, EDI, Paris, 1968 (first published in 1942).

5. Oliver C. Cox, *Caste, Class and Race*, Doubleday and Co., New York, 1948.

6. The most significant of these, or long extracts from them, are brought together in Herbert M. Hunter and Sameer Y. Abraham (eds), *Race, Class and the World System. The Sociology of Oliver C. Cox*, Monthly Review Press, New York, 1948.

7. Célestin Bouglé, *Essai sur le régime des castes*, PUF, Paris, 1989 (first published in 1908).

8. See Chapter 2.

9. See his contribution to the book he wrote with Étienne Balibar, *Race, Nation, Class. Ambiguous Identities*, trans. Chris Turner, Verso, London, 1991, p. 33.

10. See, in particular, John Rex and David Mason (eds), *Theories of Race and Ethnic Relations*, Cambridge University Press, Cambridge, 1986, which contains an extensive bibliography. This work includes articles directly concerned with the debates which interest us here by, among others, Michael Banton, John Solomos and Harold Wolpe. See also Anni Phizacklea and Robert Miles, *Labour and Racism*, Routledge and Kegan Paul, London, 1980; Robert Miles, 'Marxism versus the Sociology of Race Relations?', *Ethnic and Racial Studies*, vol. 7, no. 2, 1984, pp. 217–37, and 'Class, Race and Ethnicity. A Critique of Cox's Theory', *Ethnic and Racial Studies*, vol. 3, no. 2, 1980, pp. 169–87.

11. Pierre Ayçoberry, *The Nazi Question. An Essay on the Interpretation of National-Socialism (1922–1975)*, trans. Robert Hurley, Routledge and Kegan Paul, London, 1981.

12. Nicos Poulantzas, *Fascism and Dictatorship*, New Left Books, London, 1974.

13. Enzo Traverso, *Les Marxistes et la Question juive*, La Brèche, Montreuil, 1990, p. 245.

14. Balibar in *Race, Nation, Class*, p. 205.

15. Floya Anthias, 'Race and Class Revisited. Conceptualising Race and Ethnicity', *The Sociological Review*, vol. 38, no. 1, February 1990, pp. 19–42.

16. Alain Touraine, Michel Wieviorka and François Dubet, *The Workers' Movement*, trans. Ian Patterson, Cambridge University Press, Cambridge, 1983.

17. See Alain Touraine, *La Conscience ouvrière*, Éditions du Seuil, Paris, 1966.

18. Quoted by Philip S. Foner, *Organized Labor and the Black Worker 1619–1973*, International Publishers, New York, 1974, p. x.

19. Robert Merton, Social Theory and Social Structure, second edition, Free Press, Glencoe, 1957.

20. Cf. Norman Hill ('Blacks and the Unions', *Dissent*, spring 1989, pp. 496–500), who cites some eloquent figures: in 1987, blacks made up 14.5 per cent of trade unionists; 22.6 per cent of black workers were in trade unions as opposed to 16.3 per cent of white workers.

21. For more details, see Michel Wieviorka, *Les Juifs, la Pologne et Solidarnosc*, Denoël, Paris, 1984.

22. See Alain Touraine, François Dubet, Michel Wieviorka and Jan Strzelecki, *Solidarity*, trans. D. Denby, Cambridge University Press, Cambridge, 1983.

Chapter 10

1. See, in particular, Alain Touraine, 'Introduction à la méthode de l'intervention socio-logique', *La Méthode de l'intervention sociologique*, ADIS, Paris, 1983 pp. 11–28. For an initial elaboration of the notion of social anti-movement, see also Michel Wieviorka, *Sociétés et terrorisme*, Fayard, Paris, 1988, chapter 1.

2. See William J. Wilson, *The Declining Significance of Race*, University of Chicago Press, Chicago, 1978, and *The Truly Disadvantaged: The Inner City, the Underclass and Public Policy*, University of Chicago Press, Chicago, 1987.

3. See, for example, Nicos Poulantzas, *Classes in Contemporary Capitalism*, New Left Books, London, 1976.

4. Albert Hirschman, *Shifting Involvements: Private Interest and Public Action*, Martin Robertson, Oxford, 1982.

5. Cf. Michel Wieviorka, 'Les bases du national-populisme', *Le Débat*, September 1980, pp. 35–41.

6. John Dollard, *Caste and Class in a Southern Town*, University of Wisconsin Press, Madison, 1988, p. 446.

7. Cf. Gordon W. Allport, *The Nature of Prejudice*, Addison-Wesley, Reading, MA, 1987, chapter XV, and Yves Chevalier, *L'Antisémitisme*, Éditions du Cerf, Paris, 1988, p. 371.

8. For another distinction which is also close to our own, cf. Richard A. Schermerhorn (*Comparative Ethnic Relations: A Framework for Theory and Research*, University of Chicago Press, Chicago, 1978), who differentiates between a minimal form of racism and a maximal form, 'where the distinctions between superordinates and subordinates assume an absolute rather than a relative character, one of kind and not of degree' (pp. 73–4). Schermerhorn hesitates, however, to describe Nazi anti-semitism as the maximal form and introduces a third category here – 'residual' racism (p. 77) – to mark the totally mythical character of the Hitlerian definition of the Jewish race and the fact that this phenomenon takes us beyond the sphere of 'race relations' studies.

9. Jacob Katz, 'Misreading of Anti-Semitism', *Commentary*, no. 76, July 1983, pp. 39–44.

10. Saül Friedländer, *L'Antisémitisme nazi. Histoire d'une psychose collective*, Éditions du Seuil, Paris, 1971.

11. Cf. Paul Lendvaï, *L'Antisémitisme sans Juifs*, Fayard, Paris, 1971.

12. Victor Karady and Istvan Kémény, 'Les Juifs dans la structure des classes en Hongrie: essai sur les antécédents historiques des crises antisémites du XXe siècle', *Actes de la recherche en sciences sociales*, no. 22, June 1978, pp. 25–9, and 'Antisémitisme universitaire et concurrence de classe: la loi du numerus clausus en Hongrie entre les deux guerres', *Actes de la recherche en sciences sociales*, no. 34, September 1980, pp. 67–96.

Chapter 11

1. Léon Poliakov, *The History of Anti-Semitism*, translated by Natalie Gerardi, vol. 2, Routledge and Kegan Paul, London, 1974, chapters 10 and 11.

2. Charles Amiel, 'La "pureté de sang" en Espagne', *Études interethniques*, no. 6, 1983, pp. 27–45.

3. See, for example, Benjamin B. Ringer and Elinor R. Lawless, *Race, Ethnicity and Society*, Routledge, New York, 1989; Joe R. Fragin, *Racial and Ethnic Relations*, Prentice Hall, Englewood Cliffs, NJ, 1984; Michael Banton, *Racial and Ethnic Competition*, Cambridge University Press, Cambridge, 1983, etc. The journal referred to is *Ethnic and Racial Studies* and the remit of its research committee is to investigate relations between races, ethnic groups and minorities.

4. Anthony D. Smith, *The Ethnic Revival in the Modern World*, Cambridge University Press, Cambridge, 1981.

5. Pierre L. Van den Berghe, *The Ethnic Phenomenon*, Elsevier, New York, 1981.

6. Stephen Steinberg, *The Ethnic Myth. Race, Ethnicity and Class in America*, Beacon Press, Boston, 1989 (first published in 1981).

7. Ferdinand Tönnies, *Community and Association, Gemeinschaft und Gesellschaft*, translated and supplemented by Charles P. Loomis, Routledge and Kegan Paul, London, 1955 (German original first published in 1877).

8. Max Weber, *Economy and Society*, vol. 1, University of California Press, Berkeley/Los Angeles/London, 1978; see, in particular, chapters III–V of part two.

9. Ibid., p. 399: 'we make it our task to study the conditions and effects of a particular type of social action.'

10. See, for example, ibid., pp. 397–8: 'Time and again we find that the concept "nation" directs us to political power. Hence, the concept seems to refer – if it refers at all to a uniform phenomenon – to a specific kind of pathos which is linked to the idea of a powerful political community of people who share a common language, or religion, or common customs, or political memories; such a state may already exist or it may be desired.'

11. See the interesting account offered by Elaine M. Burgess, 'The Resurgence of Ethnicity. Myth or Reality?', *Ethnic and Racial Studies*, vol. 1, no. 3, July 1978, pp. 265–85; and also James McKay, 'An Exploratory Synthesis of Primordial and Mobilizationist Approaches to Ethnic Phenomena', *Ethnic and Racial Studies*, vol. 5, no. 4, October 1982.

12. Pierre Clastres, *Society against the State*, translated by Robert Hurley in collaboration with Abe Stein, Urizen Books, New York, p. 184.

13. See Joseph Marcus, *Social and Political History of the Jews in Poland, 1919–1939*, Mouton, Berlin/New York/Amsterdam, 1983.

14. See, for example, the analysis of the struggles around the crisis of steel production in Lorraine which Claude Durand proposes in his *Chômage et Violence*, Galilée, Paris, 1981.

15. Anthony D. Smith, 'War and Ethnicity. The Role of Warfare in the Formation, Self-Images and Cohesion of Ethnic Communities', *Ethnic and Racial Studies*, vol. 4, no. 4, October 1981.

16. See Georg Simmel, *Conflict and the Web of Group-Affiliations*, *Conflict* translated by Kurt H. Wolff, *The Web* translated by Reinhard Bendix, Free Press of Glencoe, London, 1955; Georges Sorel, *Reflections on Violence*, translated by T.E. Hulme, Collier-Macmillan, London, 1961; Frantz Fanon, *The Wretched of the Earth*, translated by Constance Farrington, Penguin, Harmondsworth, 1967.

17. Albert Memmi, *Le Racisme*, Gallimard, Paris, 1982, p. 71.

18. Cf. Michel Wieviorka, *Sociétés et Terrorisme*, Fayard, Paris, 1988, part V.

19. Robert Brijtenhuijt, 'Mouvements nationaux ou mouvements ethniques? Quelques exemples africains', read at the Journées de la Société française de sociologie, Paris, 29–30 September 1989.

20. Ernest Gellner, *Nations and Nationalism*, Basil Blackwell, Oxford, 1983, p. 124.

21. Edward Shils, 'Primordial, Personal, Sacred and Civil Ties', *British Journal of Sociology*, June 1957, pp. 130–45; Clifford Geertz, 'The Integrative Revolution: Primordial Sentiments and Civil Politics in the New States' in Geertz (ed.), *Old Societies and New States*, Free Press, New York, 1963, pp. 105–57.

22. E.P. Thompson, *The Making of the English Working Class*, Pelican, Harmondsworth, 1968.

23. Alain Touraine, *Return of the Actor: Social Theory in Postindustrial Society*, foreword by Stanley Aronowitz, translated by Myrna Godzich, University of Minnesota Press, Minneapolis, 1988, p. 81.

24. Gilles Kepel, *Le Prophète et Pharaon*, La Découverte, Paris, 1984.

25. See Michel Wieviorka, *Sociétés et terrorisme*, part 5.

26. Benedict Anderson, *Imagined Communities. Reflexions on the Origin and Spread of Nationalism*, Verso, London, 1983, p. 136; Paul Gilroy, *There Ain't No Black in the Union Jack*, Hutchinson, London, 1987, pp. 44–5.

27. Étienne Balibar and Immanuel Wallerstein, *Race, Nation, Class. Ambiguous Identities*, trans. Chris Turner, Verso, London, p. 54.

28. Ibid., p. 60.

29. A position defended, for example, by René Gallissot, *Misère de l'antiracisme*, Arcantère, Paris, 1985. And, since we have in this work made quite a number of references to Max Weber, his categorical opposition to the racial theories of his day and his scathing criticism of the arguments of Dr Ploetz, let us also recall here that he was an ardent nationalist and a member of the Pan-German League. This illustrates the radical distance which may exist between nationalism and racism.

30. Amiel, 'La "pureté de sang" en Espagne', p. 41.

31. Michael R. Marrus and Robert O. Paxton, *Vichy France and the Jews*, Basic Books, New York, 1981.

32. Marrus stresses that this fusion of the two most central circles creates a dynamic which does not carry the masses along with it: it makes organized, political action possible, but this is not the same thing; see Michael R. Marrus, 'Théorie et pratique de l'antisémitisme', *Sens*, no. 1, 1985, pp. 17–25. On this theme, see also Walter Laqueur (*The Terrible Secret. An Investigation into the Suppression of Information about Hitler's 'Final Solution'*, Weidenfeld and Nicholson, London, 1980), who shows how the destruction of the Jews by the Nazis was shrouded in secrecy for internal as well as international reasons, and Raoul Hillberg (*La Destruction des Juifs d'Europe*, Fayard, Paris, 1988), who points out that the massive massacres of Jews on the eastern front during 'mobile killing operations' led to tensions and problems of conscience within the German units involved.

Conclusion: The Unity of Racism

This conclusion to Part Three draws very largely on a note produced by Alain Touraine after reading a first version of this book. While I accept full responsibility for what is said here, it would, none the less, be impossible not to acknowledge Touraine's contribution and to thank him once again for his intellectual and personal support.

1. Arno Mayer, *Why Did the Heavens Not Darken? The 'Final Solution' in History*, Verso, London, 1990.

2. See Michel Wieviorka, 'La crise du modèle français d'intégration', *Regards sur l'actualité*, no. 161, May 1990, pp. 3–15.

3. In his speech of 28 July 1885 to the Chamber of Deputies; see Jean-Michel Gaillard, *Jules Ferry*, Fayard, Paris, 1989, p. 540.

Conclusion

1. Among many other works which we might cite, see for the USA: Phyllis A. Katz and Dalmas A. Taylor (eds), *Eliminating Racism. Profiles in Controversy*, Plenum Press, New York, 1988; for the UK: Michael Banton, *Promoting Racial Harmony*, Cambridge University Press, Cambridge, 1985.

2. Let us remind the reader that, in autumn 1989, the decision by the head of a college at Creil to ban from classes three girls wearing the Islamic headscarf gave rise to an extensive debate within the media and among politicians.

3. Michel Crozier, *On ne change pas la société par décret*, Grasset, Paris, 1979.

INDEX

Adorno, T.W. 21–3
Africa, post-colonial 111
Aigues-Mortes 140
Aix-les-Bains 128
Allport, G.W. 23 41, 47, 67, 100
America *see* United States of America (USA)
American Anthropological Association 24
American Association of Black Sociologists 59, 138
American Federation of Labour (AFL) 87
American Jewish Committee 21
American Journal of Sociology 10
Amiel, C. 102, 116
Ammon, O. 4
Anderson, B. 115
Anthias, F. 85
anthropology 29
anti-black American racism 8, 9–10, 63, 74, 100
    see also Negro, problem
anti-semitism 21, 31–3, 82
    German 5, 29–30, 78, 100–1, 116
    Orleans rumour 49–50, 52, 57
    Poland 72, 90–1
apartheid 54, 60, 61, 73–4, 76
Arab world 112
Arafat, Y. 112
Arendt, H. 26
assassination, collective 110
Ayçoberry, P. 84

Baker, R. 87
Balibar, É. 85, 115, 125
Banton, M. 49
Barker, M. 42
Basque separatist movement (ETA) 113
behaviour, defensive 109
Beilis case (1911) 75
bio-social theory of ethnic populations 103
blacks *see* anti-black American racism; Negro, problem
Boas, F. 11
Bogardus, E.S. 57
Bouglé, C. 84

Boulainvilliers, H. 83
Brijtenhuijt, R. 112
Britain *see* United Kingdom
Brotherhood of Sleeping Car Porters 88
Burgess, E.W. 55
Burke, E. 27

Cantril, H. 83
Carmichael, S. 62
Carpentras 128
caste system 12, 13, 15–16, 28
Chamberlain, H.S. 4, 117
Chevalier, Y. 35, 100
Chicago Commission on Race Relations 13
Chicago riots (1919) 74
Chicago School 55–7
Christianity 102
Clark, K.B. 59
class 83, 84, 110
    and caste 15–16
    middle 28, 97–9
    underclass 58–9, 96, 120
    working 96, 113
Clastres, P. 106
colonialism 27–8, 43, 108, 110
communal identity 102–18, 126
    communal movements
        formation 108–14
        notion of 104–8
        and social movements 113–14
    community and communal action 103–4
Comte, A. 3
concentric circles theory 117, 144
conflict, class 84
conspiracy argument 32
Cooley, C.H. 10
Cox, O. 83–4
crime 139
crisis
    industrial 109
    modernity 121–2, 125
    social 121
    social/political 68–9
    state 111